The writings of Josephus are essential to a complete and proper understanding of Jewish thought and history.

Now, for the first time, a newly edited edition of Josephus' "classic" works centers on the history of the Jewish people up to and around the time of Christ. All the information you need to know is in this extremely readable narrative . . . all the drama, the intrigue, plus all the important background information of most interest to Christians.

JOSEPHUS
THRONES OF BLOOD

**A HISTORY OF THE TIMES OF JESUS
37 B.C. TO A.D. 70**

A BARBOUR BOOK

JOSEPHUS 37 B.C. - A.D. 70

ISBN 1-55748-266-7

CONTENTS

HEROD THE GREAT

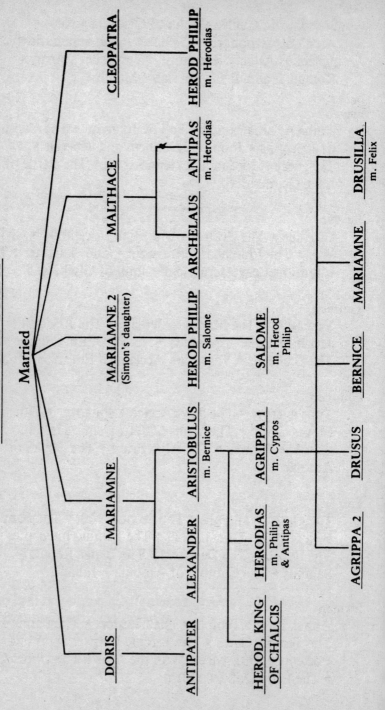

INTRODUCTION

Christian scholars are well acquainted with the works of Josephus, as are many laymen, but he has always posed problems for the average reader. The classic English translation of his works is William Whiston's, which was first published in 1738–1741. The combination of Josephus's florid style and Whiston's own complex writing produced a fascinating book, but one very hard for the average reader to wade through.

This volume is designed to be read by the average layman, not by biblical scholars. It covers the period from 37 B.C., when Herod took Jerusalem to become the king of the Jews, to A.D. 70, the year the Romans destroyed the temple and the city of Jerusalem. This is the period most interesting to Christians, who will recognize many familiar biblical names, places, and events and learn much about this period that will enhance their understanding of and appreciation for the Bible itself.

This book is a paraphrase of Whiston's translation, part *The Antiquities of the Jews* and part *The Jewish War*, combined into one chronological narrative. It should be easier to read and understand than Whiston; it flows along logically, and most of the long speeches of dubious authenticity have been summarized instead of quoted verbatim. The casual reader interested in this period should have no problem understanding what's going on.

Who Was Josephus?

Josephus was a Jerusalem Jew who was born in A.D. 37 or 38 and died about A.D. 100. His given name was Joseph ben Matthias, although he later took the Roman name Flavius Josephus. At the age of nineteen, he became a Pharisee; he served as a priest until the age of twenty-six, at which point he became involved in the Jewish rebellion against the Romans. At twenty-nine, he was the governor of Galilee, a general, and an administrator committed to the Jewish cause.

But Josephus was nothing if not practical and ambitious. He soon saw that the Romans would overpower the Jewish rebellion, did a convenient (and traitorous) flip-flop, and served the Romans for the rest of his life. At the time he wrote his histories, Josephus was more a pagan than a Jew, although he claimed otherwise.

The strong point of Josephus's works lies in the fact that he was there and personally involved in the Jewish rebellion. As far as historical facts go, he was a thorough, dependable historian. But, as with all historians, Josephus had certain biases and weak points. Readers should note that he tended to exaggerate quantities, painted his enemies worse than they were, and made himself and his friends seem better that any of them really deserved. Therefore the reader will find Titus glorified, John of Gischala vilified, and Josephus perfectly justified in deserting the Jewish cause. A little discrimination is required in the reading.

Even with these reservations, there is still no better source than Josephus for the reader who wants to know the true character of Herod the Great, what the temple and the city of Jerusalem looked like in Jesus' days, or why the Roman army was so invincible. The wealth of background material provided by Josephus is invaluable for the Christian's understanding of biblical times.

ONE

In 37 B.C. Herod defeated Antigonus, the last of the Hasmonean kings, with Rome's help, and the government of all Judea was in his hands. He promoted his supporters in Jerusalem while relentlessly punishing those who had opposed him. With Jerusalem firmly in his grasp, he proceeded to carry off all the royal ornaments and confiscate the riches of the city's citizens, heaping together a great quantity of silver and gold that he sent off to Mark Antony and his friends in Rome.

He also executed forty-five leaders of Antigonus's party and placed guards at the city gates so nothing could be carried out with the bodies of the dead, all of which were searched. Anything of value that was found was taken to the new king. Herod's greed, combined with the fact that this was a Sabbatic Year and the land was lying fallow, brought a great deal of suffering to the citizens of Judea and hard feelings toward their new king.

At first, Antony decided to keep the captured Antigonus alive in Rome, but when he heard that the Jews still supported Antigonus and hated Herod, whom he had made their king, Antony had Antigonus beheaded in Antioch, hoping to disgrace his memory and subdue the protests of the Jews.

In 43 B.C., Hyrcanus, the Jewish high priest and Hasmonean king of the Jews before Antigonus, had been captured by invading Parthians and carried off to Parthia, where King Phraates treated him with the respect and dignity due his position and his illustrious family. Hyrcanus was allowed to live unbound in a city named Babylon, which was well populated with Jews who honored him as their high priest and king — as did most of the Jews in the area.

When Hyrcanus was informed that Herod had defeated Antigonus and been granted control of all Judea, he became hopeful of returning to his country. He still felt kindly toward Herod and expected Herod to be grateful for all the help Hyrcanus had provided him in the past. He told the Jews who often came to visit him in Babylon of his desire to return to Judea. These men tried to convince Hyrcanus to stay put, reminding him that he was already being treated with the honor and respect due a high priest and king. They also warned him that men change when they attain power and that Herod was unlikely to reward Hyrcanus for his past kindnesses; nevertheless, Hyrcanus still longed to return to Judea.

Soon a letter arrived from Herod, urging Hyrcanus to ask Phraates and the local Jews for his freedom. Herod promised to share his royal authority with Hyrcanus if he returned, maintaining that he only wanted to repay Hyrcanus for his past favors, now that he had the power to do so.

In addition to this letter, Herod also sent Saramallas as ambassador to Phraates — along with many presents — asking Phraates not to hinder his gratitude toward Hyrcanus.

In truth, Herod's zeal for Hyrcanus's return had nothing to do with gratitude. Having just been made governor of Judea with no just claim, he was justifiably afraid of being overthrown. He needed Hyrcanus, who had a valid claim to the throne, close by, where he could control him.

The king of Parthia gave Hyrcanus permission to leave; the reluctant Jews of Babylon provided him with financial assistance. Full of assurance, Hyrcanus returned to Herod, who received him with all possible respect. He gave Hyrcanus the upper place at all public meetings, set him above all the rest at feasts, called him "father," and tried by all means to avoid arousing any suspicions in Hyrcanus. Hyrcanus was totally deceived.

The High Priesthood

Meanwhile, afraid to appoint any well-known person to the powerful position of high priest, Herod sent for Ananelus, an obscure priest from Babylon, and bestowed the position on him, thereby igniting a rebellion within his own family.

Alexandra, Hyrcanus's daughter (and Herod's mother-in-law), was highly incensed that the position did not go to her son Aristobulus (Herod's young brother-in-law). Understanding the Roman power structure quite well and being an outspoken woman, she wrote to Cleopatra and asked her to intercede with Antony and obtain the high priesthood for Aristobulus.

Antony was slow in granting this request, but his friend Dellius happened to come to Judea on business, where he met Alexandra and her two children, Aristobulus and Mariamne (Herod's wife). Seeing that all three were extremely attractive, he encouraged Alexandra to send portraits of her children to Antony, who would surely grant her any wish, once he saw her lovely children.

Dellius's aim in all of this was not to obtain the high priesthood for Aristobulus, but simply to provide sexual pleasures for Antony, who was well-known for indulging his desires. Antony decided it would be wiser not to send for Mariamne. She was, after all, his friend Herod's wife, and he would no doubt hear from Cleopatra, if he were that bold. However, he did politely request Aristobulus's presence.

Herod, who knew Antony well, thought it unwise to send him a handsome sixteen-year-old from a prominent family. Since Aristobulus was also a legitimate heir to the Jewish throne, Herod told Antony the people would rise up in revolt if the boy were sent out of the country (it was also to Herod's advantage to keep the boy close and under supervision).

13

Once this matter was settled, Herod's wife, Mariamne, vehemently set upon him to restore the high priesthood to her brother, Aristobulus. Since this would keep the boy at home, Herod agreed. He called all his friends together and told them Alexandra had conspired with Cleopatra against his authority; nevertheless, he would do the right thing and make Aristobulus high priest. Ananelus had only been appointed because the boy was so young, he told them.

Alexandra, delighted by the outcome and fearful of Herod's accusations, promptly apologized, assuring Herod that she and Aristobulus were loyal to him. Herod accepted, and all was forgiven — on the surface.

So Herod took the high priesthood away from Ananelus, who was not from Judea but was one of the Jews who had been taken beyond the Euphrates as a captive. Herod's act, although necessary to restore peace to his own household, was plainly illegal. In all of Jewish history, this was only the third time a high priest had been removed from office by a civil authority.

Aristobulus's Murder

Seemingly, all was well within Herod's family, although he still distrusted Alexandra, believing she would happily make trouble for him anytime she found the opportunity. To keep her under control, he commanded her to live in the palace and keep out of public affairs. Her personal guards were so "careful" that nothing in her private life was unknown to Herod.

This lack of freedom tried Alexandra's patience, causing her to hate Herod more and more. A woman of great pride, she would have preferred almost anything to being deprived of her freedom of speech and being a virtual prisoner of her son-in-law. Therefore she sent to Cleopatra, complaining of her circumstances. Cleopatra urged her to come to Egypt with Aristobulus and live with her, an idea Alexandra readily adopted.

The problem was in escaping from the palace, for Alexandra knew Herod would never willingly let her go. She had two coffins made — one for her and one for her son — and arranged to be carried out of the palace during the night to a waiting ship bound for Egypt.

Unfortunately, one of Alexandra's servants spoke of the plan to the wrong person, and word immediately got back to Herod, who caught Alexandra and Aristobulus in the act of trying to escape in the coffins. Although he would have preferred to be severe with them right then, he pretended generosity and forgiveness, knowing Cleopatra would not stand by while Alexandra was accused and punished. But the attempted escape sealed Aristobulus's fate; although Herod would have to wait until this event was forgotten, he determined that young Aristobulus would, in due time, die.

Soon it was time for the Feast of the Tabernacles. Aristobulus, now seventeen years old, went up to the altar to offer the sacrifices as the high priest. As he performed the sacred offices, he seemed extremely attractive to everyone at the service, tall for his age, and obviously from an important family. The crowd's outspoken admiration of Aristobulus — and their warm memories of his heroic grandfather — were too noticeable for Aristobulus's good.

At the end of the festival, Herod joined Alexandra and Aristobulus at a feast they hosted in Jericho, playing in a childish way with the boy and joining in the general celebration. It being hotter than normal that day, in the evening some of Herod's servants and acquaintances dove into the large fish ponds by the house; soon, encouraged by Herod, Aristobulus joined them. Under cover of darkness, Herod's appointed murderers dunked Aristobulus as though in play; he never came up alive. After one year as the high priest, seventeen-year-old Aristobulus was dead. Ananelus returned to the office he had lost one year before.

The Aftermath of Aristobulus's Death

Hearing of Aristobulus's death, the whole city of Jerusalem fell into deep mourning. Alexandra was, of course, the most deeply affected of all, her sorrow made even deeper by the knowledge that her son had been murdered. She couldn't accuse Herod without endangering herself, but she often thought of suicide. Finally, she resolved to survive at all costs, for the sake of future vengeance.

Herod did everything in his power to keep people from suspecting him. His obvious grief, which may have actually been genuine after the fact, consoled the women of the family to some degree, but didn't fool Alexandra in the least. As usual, she confided in Cleopatra, who persuaded Antony to look into the matter.

Antony commanded Herod to come to Laodicea and defend himself. Herod had no choice but to go, so he appointed his uncle, Joseph, procurator in his absence. Before leaving, Herod privately instructed Joseph to kill Mariamne if he should be executed by Antony. Although he told Joseph he gave the command because he loved his wife and feared Antony would harm her, in reality Herod knew Antony was attracted to his wife and didn't want her to remarry anyone — especially Antony.

In the course of tending to the kingdom's business, Joseph saw Mariamne and the palace women frequently. Each time he did, he took pains to assure them of Herod's love — reassurance that was scorned, especially by Alexandra. Finally, hoping to convince them, Joseph told them of Herod's final order. To him, it offered proof that Herod could not bear to be separated, even in death, from those he loved. The women saw it differently.

Soon rumors began to circulate that Antony had killed Herod. The women immediately began planning their escape to the Roman legion guarding the city. Before the plan was complete, letters arrived from Herod assuring them all was well. Antony had decided for Herod and told Cleopatra to keep out of Judean affairs, pacifying her with control of Celesyria (although it was Judea she coveted).

As soon as he returned home, Herod's sister, Salome, and his mother told him of the women's escape plans. Salome, who hated Mariamne, falsely accused Joseph of being Mariamne's lover.

There can be no doubt that Herod loved his wife. Tormented by jealousy, he still gave her a chance to defend herself, which

16

she did very convincingly. In the midst of Herod's apology for doubting her, Mariamne, who should have known better, asked him: "Yet was not that command thou gavest, that if any harm came to thee from Antony, I, who had been no occasion of it, should perish with thee, a sign of thy love to me?"

Herod flew into a rage. If Joseph had confided a private order to Mariamne, there *must* have been something going on between them! Only Herod's love for Mariamne saved her life; Joseph was killed with no chance to defend himself. As for Alexandra, she was bound and kept in custody as the instigator of the whole affair.

Cleopatra in Judea

Cleopatra had thrown the affairs of Syria into confusion. Taking advantage of Antony's infatuation with her, she successfully entreated him to take several kingdoms away from their rulers and give them to her.

She was a naturally covetous woman, stopping short of nothing to gain whatever she desired. At this point, she had already poisoned her fifteen-year-old brother to keep the throne of Egypt in her possession and had her sister Arsinoe slain. Cleopatra had no qualms about plundering temples and tombs for their riches; no place was too holy or too profane, if it could contribute to her wealth. Yet all she owned failed to satisfy her; she constantly petitioned Antony for more. While traveling through Syria with him, she contrived to gain more kingdoms for herself, including those of Judea and Arabia.

Antony seemed powerless to refuse her requests, yet her injustices caused him enough shame to prevent him from totally giving in. Instead, he took parts of each country away from its governor and presented them to her. All the cities within the river Eleutherus, as far as Egypt, were bestowed on Cleopatra, with the exceptions of Tyre and Sidon, which were traditionally free.

After obtaining all she could from Antony on his expedition to Armenia, Cleopatra turned back through Apania and Damascus, into Judea, where Herod met her.

While they were together, Cleopatra, not bothing to be at all discreet about her intentions, attempted to seduce Herod. Perhaps she really did feel passion for him; more likely, she was trying to ensnare him. Herod, however, felt no affection for Cleopatra, knowing her to be a troublemaker, and was revolted by her advances. He flatly turned her proposal down, then called his friends together for some much-needed advice.

As far as Herod was concerned, it would be to everyone's advantage — even Antony's — if he killed Cleopatra then and there. Luckily, his friends were able to convince Herod he had nothing to gain and everything to lose from murdering her. They showed him that simply rejecting her advances would make him look virtuous and heroic, which was the proper stance for a king. So Herod treated Cleopatra kindly, gave her the proper amount of gifts, and conducted her on her way home to Egypt.

War With Arabia

In the seventh year of his reign (31 b.c.), Herod prepared to go to war against the ungrateful king of Arabia. At the same time, Octavian and Antony were preparing to fight each other for control of the Roman Empire at Actium.

Herod, having ruled a fruitful country and collected its taxes for seven years, was able to raise and equip a strong army, which he led off in support of Antony. Hearing of Herod's plans, Antony reassured him he did not need his military assistance. Instead, he sent a message to Herod commanding him to punish the king of Arabia, having heard from both Herod and Cleopatra how dangerous and unreliable the king had become.

This was exactly what Cleopatra had hoped for, thinking it to her own advantage that these two kings do each other as much harm as possible. (There could be more land in it for her, if they destroyed each other.)

When his army was ready, Herod marched to Diospolis, where they were met by the Arabians, whom they defeated handily. Hearing that another army of Arabians was gathered at Cana, in Celesyria (now Cleopatra's territory), Herod marched there, deciding to make camp near Cana until his army was rested enough to attack. His soldiers, encouraged by their victory in Diospolis, urged Herod to attack immediately instead of encamping, so he led them on to rout the Arabians, who would have been totally destroyed if Athenio, Cleopatra's general, had not suddenly joined the battle.

Athenio had previously decided to watch the battle, reserving his forces for use only if it appeared the Jews would win. He attacked the tired Jewish army, which thought the battle had already been won, slaughtering many. Losses were particularly heavy in rough terrain, where the horses could not be used and the Arabians had the advantage of knowing the land.

After this defeat, Herod was reduced to making guerrilla raids on the Arabians, avoiding pitched battles until he rebuilt his army.

Then an unusual and destructive earthquake hit Judea, killing large numbers of livestock and about 10,000 people. The army itself, camped in the open, suffered no physical damage but was disheartened by the news of death and destruction coming from their homes. Ambassadors were sent out to make peace with the Arabians. The Arabians, certain the Jews could now be defeated, slaughtered their ambassadors and attacked; the Jews lost all hope and became totally demoralized.

Herod was not willing to lose by default. He rallied his army by speaking to its leaders and then to the men themselves, convincing them of the righteousness of their cause in God's eyes. Seeing the morale of the army greatly improved by his words, Herod offered the sacrifices required by law, marched over Jordan, and pitched camp near the enemy. A successful skirmish over a castle further encouraged the men, who then attacked the Arabian bulwark itself, causing the Arabians to panic and lose 5,000 men. The remainder of the Arabian army barricaded itself within the bulwark. Not able to penetrate their defenses, Herod camped around the bulwark until thirst forced the Arabians to sue for peace, then refused all terms. In five days, 4,000 Arabians surrendered; the rest of the force decided to fight its way out, losing 7,000 more before surrendering and accepting Herod as the new king of Arabia.

The Death of Hyrcanus

Herod was very prosperous and not easily endangered until Octavian's defeat of Antony made it probable that he would be punished for his longtime friendship and support of Antony.

Feeling suddenly insecure, Herod realized that the only person left in Judea of royal stature and breeding was Hyrcanus, who would certainly inherit the kingdom if Herod were deposed or killed.

Hyrcanus had never shown any inclination or desire for power. In all his more than eighty years, he had never been ambitious for himself, simply taking whatever fortune bestowed on him and being satisfied with that. But his daughter, Alexandra, was a different matter.

The events that followed are in dispute: Herod's commentaries disagree with those of other historians of the time. Whether Herod laid a trap for Hyrcanus or Hyrcanus was finally prodded into action by his ambitious daughter, contact was made with Malchus, the governor of Arabia, who promised Hyrcanus and his family refuge. Herod heard of these plans (or manufactured them), accused Hyrcanus of treason, and had him executed.

Hyrcanus had endured many changes of fortune during his long life: high priest for nine years; king for three months; betrayal by his brother; king for forty additional years; captive of the Persians. Worst of all, he died an undeserved death at the hands of Herod, whom he had always supported.

Herod Before Caesar

As soon as he had eliminated Hyrcanus, Herod prepared to go to Octavian. Since he could not trust Alexandra not to overthrow him while he was away, he turned the government over to his brother Pheroras and sent his family off to the fortress of Masada. Mariamne, who could not live with Herod's mother and sister because of their mutual hatred, was sent to her mother, Alexandra, at Alexandrium, under the care of Herod's treasurer, Joseph, and Sohemus of Iturea. He left these two men with orders to kill both women if any harm came to him and see that the kingdom was preserved for his sons and Pheroras.

These preparations completed, Herod hurried off to meet Octavian at Rhodes. He came before him without his crown, but gave up nothing else. In no way denying his friendship and support of Antony or groveling for forgiveness, Herod maintained he had only done for Antony what friendship required; perhaps he had not even done enough. Now he offered that same friendship and devotion to Octavian.

Impressed by Herod's frankness and being a naturally generous person, Octavian forgave Herod and returned his kingdom to him. Herod gratefully escorted Octavian on his way to Egypt, presenting him with many gifts and supplying his army for their upcoming invasion of Egypt. His generosity was actually more than he could afford, but it did secure him Octavian's trust. Judea was once again firmly in Herod's hands.

Herod and Mariamne

Herod returned to Judea to find his household in an uproar. First, Mariamne and her mother were well aware that they were not being kept at Alexandrium solely for their protection. Second, Mariamne once again learned of Herod's plans for her if he were to die. While he was gone, Mariamne decided it would be impossible for her to continue living with Herod.

Unsuspecting, Herod rushed to his wife to share his good news, only to find her full of resentment and hatred toward him. Worse yet, she was no longer even pretending to love him, but openly showed her scorn. Herod wavered in despair, torn between his love for Mariamne and his overwhelming anger at her. Herod's sister, Salome, and their mother naturally took this opportunity to tell Herod lie after lie about his wife; still Herod could not bring himself to act, knowing how much he would suffer from Mariamne's death.

Soon news arrived that Octavian had taken Egypt and both Antony and Cleopatra were dead (30 B.C.). Herod left his family behind to join Octavian in Egypt, where Octavian restored the lands taken from him by Cleopatra and added to that the lands of Gadara, Hippos, and Samaria, as well as the towns of Gaza, Anthedon, Joppa, and Strato's Tower. Herod accompanied Caesar as far as Antioch, then returned to his family.

Herod knew he had been fortunate to win the love of beautiful Mariamne, who was a chaste and faithful wife, even if she was contentious and never hesitated to speak her mind to him. She did take advantage of his love for her; still, he managed to laugh off most of her barbed comments, even those about the low birth station of his mother and sister. He loved her madly, but now she had nothing but hatred for him. They lived in this uneasy state for a year after Herod's return from Caesar.

Finally, everything came to a head. Herod lay down for a noontime rest one day, calling for Mariamne. She came as ordered, but refused to join him in his bed. Instead, she berated him for causing the deaths of her grandfather (Hyrcanus) and brother (Aristobulus).

Salome, hearing that Herod was more upset than usual with his wife, sent in his cupbearer to tell Herod that Mariamne had ordered him to give Herod a love potion. Herod seemed pleased at this turn of events until the cupbearer confided that he didn't know what was in the potion and therefore thought it best to warn Herod. The obvious conclusion, to which Herod violently jumped, was that Mariamne was attempting to poison him.

He at least allowed his wife a trial, building his case around the complete fabrication of the nonexistent poisoned love potion. Herod was so furious at his wife that the court readily agreed she should be put to death. Although there was some talk of simply imprisoning her, Salome convinced her brother that the citizens of Judea would rise up if Mariamne were locked away; she had to die.

Mariamne's mother, Alexandra, afraid that she, too, would lose her life, immediately came to Herod's defense, publicly reproaching her "ungrateful" daughter. Her change of heart fooled no one, especially her doomed daughter, who was ashamed of her mother's actions.

Thus Mariamne, a woman of excellent character, chastity, and beauty — but also one who lacked moderation and too often became contentious — died. She trusted too much that Herod's love would protect her from his anger.

As he had feared, Herod suffered enormously from Mariamne's death, for he truly did love her. He would frequently call out for her or send servants for her, weeping and disconsolate. Affairs of state were ignored. A pestilence that killed great numbers of people was seen as God's punishment for Mariamne's murder. Herod fled to the desert to escape his torment, only to come down with a serious illness and finally go mad with grief.

At this point, Alexandra was living in Jerusalem. She heard of Herod's condition and attempted to gain control of Jerusalem's fortifications: one in the city and the other belonging to the temple. She claimed she was only looking after the interests of Herod's heirs, but those in control of the forts immediately sent word to Herod of Alexandra's schemes. He rallied from his grief long enough to order his mother-in-law's immediate execution and the deaths of some friends who might lay claim to the throne. Now there was no one left alive from the old royal family. Judea was uncontestably Herod's, but at great personal cost.

TWO

Now that there was no one left of the old royal house to oppose him or lead the people in rebellion, Herod turned away from the customs of the Jews, introducing foreign practices and causing the people to neglect their ancient religious observances. He built a theater in Jerusalem and a great amphitheater on the plain, and held games there in honor of Caesar every five years, bringing men from every nation to take part. Inscriptions of Caesar's great triumphs and trophies of his conquered nations, all adorned in the purest gold and silver, filled the theater. He also collected wild animals such as lions to fight one another or men who were condemned to death.

To the Jews, this was outright blasphemy. The trophies of war offended them the most, since they were seen as images and it was against Jewish law to pay honors to any image. Herod overcame this particular complaint by showing the city's leaders that the trophies were nothing more than pieces of wood beneath their gold and silver ornaments.

Although most of the people were pacified by this, some still believed Herod's new customs would bring grief to the nation. Ten of these men banded together to make an attempt on Herod's life, going armed to the theater and hoping to take him by surprise. Just as he was about to leave for the theater, one of Herod's many spies heard of the conspiracy and warned him, so Herod returned to his palace and had the ten brought before him. When they were accused, they made no denials but peacefully surrendered their daggers, claiming they were acting to uphold the Jewish laws. All ten were tortured to death.

Soon the spy who had discovered the conspiracy was seized by some of the people and not only killed, but pulled to pieces and thrown to the dogs. Although many people saw the incident, no one would reveal who was responsible until some women who were present were tortured until they spoke. Herod not only executed the killers themselves, but also every member of their families.

Since Herod had now fortified his palace and rebuilt the temple fortress he renamed Antonia, he now proceeded to fortify Samaria, a day's journey from Jerusalem, renaming it Sebaste. He continually built and rebuilt fortresses for his own glory, filling the nation with guards to help keep the populace in order.

The Famine and Cesarea

In the years 23 and 22 B.C., drought and famine came to Judea and Syria, causing widespread sickness and death. Even Herod was affected. Short of money because he had spent it on his many building projects and unable to collect taxes from his starving citizens, he looked for another way of alleviating the area's suffering.

To raise money to buy wheat, Herod plundered his castle of its gold and silver, then sent his wealth to Petronius, the prefect of Egypt, who provided wheat in return. Herod, being sure his subjects knew their relief came from his own pockets, distributed the food in a generous and equitable manner to all Judea. He also provided winter clothing for those who needed it, since most of the livestock had died or been consumed and there was no wool available.

Once his own subjects were taken care of, Herod provided seed and farm workers to his neighbors the Syrians. With their fruitful soil, the Syrians were then able to grow enough food to feed both countries. Through Herod's efforts, no one in the area was left destitute, which gained him much respect from other rulers and, for the first time, the love of his own people.

The famine under control, Herod went back to his building, raising a palace for himself in the upper city. He also fell in love again, this time with the daughter of Simon, a priest of Jerusalem. Simon was not of high enough status to permit this marriage, so Herod promptly deposed Jesus the son of Phabet and made Simon high priest before marrying his daughter.

After his wedding, Herod built another citadel on a hill about seven and one-half miles from Jerusalem. The fortress, ringed by circular towers, was reached by two hundred steps of polished stone. Within the castle Herod built rich, secure apartments; outside, around the bottom, he built houses. The whole complex was naturally arid, so water was piped in from long distances.

Although he refrained from doing so in Judea itself because the Jews would not permit their laws to be so flouted, Herod continued to build magnificent cities with Greek-style temples and theaters throughout his kingdom.

One such project was the rebuilding of Strato's Tower, which he renamed Cesarea. The city itself was wonderful, but the harbor was its most impressive feature. The city, located in Phoenicia between Joppa and Dora, was not a natural port, due to heavy seas that beat on it from the south. To make an artificial harbor, Herod placed huge stones into over one hundred feet of water, each stone over fifty feet long, eighteen feet wide, and nine feet thick. In this manner, he constructed a two-hundred-foot-wide mole to absorb the force of the waves and provide a sheltered harbor. Arches were built as living quarters for the sailors, and a great quay ran around the entire harbor; the entrance to the harbor was on the north, where the seas were the calmest. The harbor also boasted a great white temple that could be seen from miles at sea.

Another important feature of the city was its vast underground vault system, which allowed goods to be easily transported between the harbor and the city. This system of vaults also collected the city's waste and rainwater and was so constructed that the tides cleaned it daily. The entire project took Herod twelve years to complete.

Herod's Temple

In 19 B.C. Herod made plans to enlarge the temple of Jerusalem, which was to be his greatest work. To obtain the support of the people for this project, Herod addressed them directly, reminding them that Solomon's original temple was ninety feet taller than the current temple, which was built after the Jews returned from Babylon. The people were afraid that Herod would tear down their temple and then find himself unable to complete the expensive one he had planned, but he assured them he would not touch the existing temple until everything needed to rebuild was assembled.

In preparation for the building, Herod assembled 1,000 wagons to transport the needed stones, chose 10,000 skilled workmen, and instructed priests in the arts of stone cutting and carpentry so they could construct the inner temple itself.

The old temple foundation was dismantled and a new one laid for a temple 150 feet long and 180 feet high. The temple was built of white stones, each 37.5 feet long, 12 feet high, and about 18 feet wide. The temple doors were of the same height as the temple, adorned with veils embroidered with purple flowers. Over the doors, but under the top of the temple, spread a golden vine, its branches hanging down from a great height.

The temple and its enclosures were built on the hill that Solomon had totally enclosed with massive walls and made level at the top; the hilltop was an eighth of a mile long on each of its four sides. Solomon's original colonnade still enclosed the eastern section of the grounds.

On the north side of the grounds was the already existing fortified tower of Antonia. In the western quarter of the temple enclosure there were four gates. The first led to the king's palace via an enclosure over the valley between the palace and the temple hill. Two other gates led to the outskirts of the city, while the last led down the valley and back up again, to the other part of the city.

The south quarter of the enclosure contained gates in the center and the new royal cloisters, which towered above the valley below. This cloister contained four rows of pillars so massive that it took three men to reach completely around one of them; the cloister contained a total of 162 pillars. Three walkways were formed by the rows of pillars: The two outside ones were each 30 feet wide, 50 feet tall, and 660 feet long, while the middle walkway, taller than the outside ones, measured 100 feet tall by 45 feet wide by 660 feet long.

These colonnades and fortifications made up the first temple enclosure. The second enclosure, a few steps above the first, was a stone wall bearing an inscription forbidding any foreigner, under pain of death, from entering. This enclosure had three gates on its south wall and three on its north. The east wall contained one large gate, through which the pure and their wives might enter, although the women could go no further than the Court of Women.

Still further inward was the Court of the Israelites, where the men might enter, while beyond that was the Court of the Priests. The temple itself was within the Court of the Priests, with the altar before it for sacrifices and burnt offerings.

Herod could not enter the temple itself, because he was not a priest, but he built the cloisters and the outer enclosures over a period of eight years. The temple itself was built by the priests in a year and a half.

A secret passage was built from Antonia to the eastern gate of the inner temple, over which Herod erected a tower, so he could reach the temple underground and guard against any plans of sedition that might be made there.

It is also reported that during the time the temple itself was being built, it never rained during the daytime, but showered at night, so the work was not slowed down.

Upon the temple's completion, a great celebration was held, during which Herod himself sacrificed 300 oxen to God. The temple celebration happened to coincide with the celebration of Herod's inauguration, which made the occasion even more illustrious and extravagant.

Herod's Sons Return

In order to punish thieves who were disrupting his land, Herod enacted a new law, under which thieves were forced to leave the country and live under foreigners.

Not only was this an extremely harsh punishment, it also violated Jewish law. Jewish law required a thief to repay his victim fourfold. If he could not repay, he could be sold into slavery, but not to non-Jews, and he had to be released after six years. Under Herod's law, there was no opportunity to repay, no chance of remaining in Jewish hands, no hope of ever returning. Despite the outcry, Herod's law was enacted, causing the Jews to hate him even more than before.

Herod now sailed to Rome to see Caesar and visit his two sons living there. Since the boys were done with their studies, Caesar sent them home with their father, where they were warmly received by the people of Judea. Soon Salome and others who had told Herod lies and caused Mariamne's death began to fear what would happen to them when one of Mariamne's sons became king. To protect themselves, they passed rumors throughout the country, saying the boys wanted nothing to do with their mother's murderer. As they planned, Herod soon heard the rumors, which, since they were built on the fact that Herod did murder Mariamne, angered him. But Herod's affection for the boys seemed to outweigh his suspicions for the time being, and he arranged their marriages. Aristobulus married Bernice, Salome's daughter; Alexander married Glaphyra, the daughter of Archelaus, king of Cappadocia.

Salome continued in her attempts to discredit Aristobulus and Alexander, aided by Pheroras, Herod's brother, who hoped to obtain the kingdom if the boys were eliminated. Although the citizens of the city were fond of the boys and recognized they were not as skilled in politics as Salome, she was so clever that most eventually came to believe her accusations.

On their part, the boys erred by being too frank and open about their feelings, admitting sadness at their mother's unjust death and accusing their enemies openly until their anger seemed to endanger Herod.

When he returned from a trip abroad, Pheroras and Salome immediately warned Herod he was in danger from his sons, adding that they had made an alliance with Archelaus, Alexander's father-in-law, the king of Cappadocia. By now, Herod was beginning to think he might have been better off living a private life with a happy family instead of the rich life of a king with a miserable home life.

As a warning to his two sons by Mariamne, Herod brought his eldest son, Antipater, into his court, thinking they might not be as dangerous if the crown was not clearly in their futures. Antipater, a shrewd man, soon took over the rumor spread by Salome, carefully avoiding any suspicion that he might be involved.

As they became more and more disturbed, the boys began to harm their own cause by openly lamenting the fate of their mother and themselves and reproaching their father for his unfairness in front of their friends. This only made Herod elevate Antipater even higher and bring his mother (Doris) to his court. Herod wrote to Caesar in praise of Antipater, then sent him to Octavian with many presents, giving everyone the impression Antipater was to be his heir. Although Antipater was warmly received by Herod's friends in Rome, he feared Alexander and Aristobulus would benefit from his absence, so he kept up his campaign of lies, convincing Herod he was in danger of being murdered.

By now Herod was totally taken in; he took his sons and brought them before Caesar for judgment, claiming they were planning to take his life and steal his kingdom. Totally innocent and taken aback by the charges, the boys hesitated in defending themselves. Caesar, who knew something of what was going on, did not take their silence as an admission of guilt, because he realized they were shy and inexperienced; others in the court also showed the boys sympathy. Alexander finally answered his father's charges, rightly maintaining they had

31

done nothing wrong and encouraging Herod, if he had any actual proof of their plotting against him, to do whatever he thought necessary.

By the time Alexander had finished, Caesar and his court were firmly on the boys' side. Caesar dismissed Herod's charges, although he warned the boys to show their father the respect he was due, which they promptly did, reuniting the family. Antipater, a clever man, pretended to be delighted by the outcome.

Upon returning to Judea, Herod spoke at the temple about his trip and its outcome. He commanded everyone in his court and in the crowd to put all bad feelings behind them and accept the order of succession he proposed: Antipater first, then Alexander and Aristobulus. In the meantime, he was still king, and he expected everyone's loyalty.

Herod the Benefactor

In 9 B.C., after ten years of work, Cesarea Sebaste was completed and dedicated with extensive games and expensive celebrations. Following this, Herod erected another city on the plain of Capharsaba, which he named Antipatris for his father, Antipater. A new city above Jericho was named Cyprus for his mother. In the Jericho Valley, he erected the city of Phasaelus in honor of his brother.

Herod's generosity extended outside Judea, to every city he visited, including those in Syria and Greece. Whenever a city lacked revenue for its public works, Herod gladly made up the difference. He built Apollo's temple at Rhodes at his own expense and paid to repair the city's fleet of ships. The inhabitants of Nicopolis (at Actium) and Antioch received most of their public buildings from Herod. In addition, he took responsibility for the support and management of the Greek Olympic games.

Even those who hated Herod had to admit he was a generous man. At the same time, he was severe and cruel when it came to his subjects and his family. Being ambitious for personal honor, he was inclined to be generous when there was an opportunity for a memorial to his name. This self-seeking generosity was, however, beyond his means, which made him harsh toward his subjects. Those in court who suffered under Herod often did so because he wanted all honor for himself. Being generous and giving honor to those above him, he expected no less in return from those below him.

However, Jewish custom and law could not grant Herod the honor he so badly wanted. To the Jews, righteousness was preferred above glory. His subjects were forbidden by law from flattering their king with statues, temples, and public performances. Herod and the Jews could find no way to satisfy each other's needs.

Herod the Grave Robber

Herod had recently spent vast amounts of money in building cities and was again short of funds. Knowing that Hyrcanus had once robbed David's tomb of 3,000 silver talents (225,000 pounds of silver) and believing even more than that was left behind, he decided to make the attempt for himself.

One night he opened the tomb and went in, accompanied only by his most faithful friends. They found no coins but did find and take away golden furniture and other precious goods. Herod wanted to search the tomb more thoroughly by going farther in, even as far as the bodies of David and Solomon, but it's said that two of his guards were killed by a flame that burst out upon them. Herod, terribly frightened, ran out of the tomb and promptly had a white stone monument built at its mouth, hoping to lessen God's anger and retribution.

Herod's family troubles worsened after his grave robbing. Whether it was divine vengeance or bad luck, his family broke out in civil war. Alexander and Aristobulus, now below Antipater in status, although their mother was from a better family than his, could not bear the dishonor they felt they were suffering. Glaphyra, Alexander's new wife, hated Salome, who returned the feeling. Even the king's brother, Pheroras, couldn't keep out of trouble. Married to a servant woman he loved deeply, he rejected two of Herod's daughters when Herod offered them to him as wives.

Herod never had one quiet hour or one day without new quarrels breaking out. Salome continued to hate Alexander and Aristobulus, turning her own daughter against Aristobulus, to whom she had just been married. Things got even worse when Pheroras told Alexander that Herod had designs on Glaphyra, Alexander's new bride — information that had been fed him by Salome. The jealous boy spoke directly to Herod about this accusation.

Herod was about at the end of his rope; now they were lying about *his* honor! He sent for his brother, Pheroras, and demanded an explanation, which was, of course, that Salome had told him these things. Salome denied saying any such thing, tearing her hair, beating her breast, playing the wronged woman very well, even though the women in the court knew she was lying. At last Herod, sick of them all, sent Salome and Pheroras out of his sight and commended Alexander for coming directly to him with the report. For once, it was Salome's reputation that suffered from her lies.

Family Chaos

Herod's family troubles now spread to the palace servants and outsiders. Eunuchs and servants were tortured for any information they might have of Alexander's supposed plot against his father; some of them took the opportunity to denounce others for personal reasons, then fell under suspicion themselves.

The affairs of the palace were in such disorder that Herod forbade many of his old friends to see him, feeling he could not act freely when they were present. All this time, Antipater urged his father on to even more tortures. Alexander's young friends were put to torture, many to death, but no concrete evidence could be found against him.

Alexander would not stoop to denying the false accusations against him; in fact, he wrote letters to Herod boasting of his treason and implicating all his own enemies, including Pheroras (Herod's brother) and Salome! Perhaps he was trying to shame his father for believing the outrageous lies against him.

Archelaus, king of Cappadocia and father of Alexander's wife, arrived in Jerusalem to mediate between father and son. Instead of defending Alexander, Archelaus tried another approach, taking Herod's part, offering to dissolve his daughter's marriage and even put her to death if she knew of a plot without telling Herod. Herod soon found himself defending Alexander to Archelaus. As Herod calmed down, Archelaus began to blame Alexander's friends for corrupting him, adding that he suspected Herod's brother more than his son.

Pheroras was convinced to admit his own part in passing rumors about Alexander, and Herod, realizing the boy was innocent, reconciled with him.

Herod Loses Caesar's Friendship

While Herod had been in Rome accusing his sons before Caesar, about forty Trachonite robbers took refuge in Syria and used that country as a base for raids into Judea and Celesyria. On his return to Judea, Herod appealed to the Roman governors of Syria, asking them to punish the robbers, who now numbered about one thousand and were laying waste to his land. With the governors' permission, Herod led an army into Syria and attacked one of the robbers' strongholds.

Meanwhile, the king of Syria had gone to Rome and became friendly with Octavian. When news reached him of Herod's attack, he protested to Caesar, who immediately asked Herod's friends in Rome if the story were true: Had Herod led an army into Syria? Herod's friends, admitting he had, were given no opportunity to explain the need for his actions.

Octavian sent a letter to Herod, the gist of which was that where before Caesar had treated Herod as a friend, from now on he would be treated as a subject. Caesar would receive none of the ambassadors Herod sent to him. Herod had lost the friendship of the most powerful man in the world.

The Deaths of Alexander and Aristobulus

Herod's distrust and hatred of Alexander and Aristobulus increased to such a degree that he encouraged men to speak against them and tortured many others until they said whatever Herod wanted to hear. Herod produced some of those who had been tortured before a crowd at Jericho and had them denounce his sons; the angry crowd stoned some of the witnesses to death and had to be restrained from doing the same to Alexander and Aristobulus.

The young men, kept under guard, were ordered to write down all the things they had done against their father. They denied making any plans against Herod but admitted that they planned to run away to Archelaus, who promised to send them to Rome.

Although Herod was still out of favor with Caesar, he needed his permission to kill his sons, so he sent two more ambassadors off with letters containing the charges against the boys. When they arrived in Rome, the ambassadors discovered that Herod's friend Nicolaus had finally been able to explain Herod's attack on Syria; they delivered the letters.

In reply, Caesar gave Herod permission to kill the boys if he could prove they had plotted against him. If they had only planned to run away, all Herod could do was admonish them. He suggested Herod assemble some people of authority in Berytus and let them decide what should be done.

While he was out of favor with Octavian, Herod had refrained from acting rashly out of anger; now he became bold. He assembled 150 assessors in Berytus and went before them, not allowing his sons to be present or to speak in their own defense. He vehemently denounced them as planning his murder, not permitting any verification of his testimony but asserting on his own authority that he was telling the truth.

The assessors, realizing this was not an assembly designed for getting to the truth or effecting a reconciliation, confirmed Herod's authority to punish the boys. Some spoke against killing them, but no prohibition was placed on Herod's actions.

Herod sailed back to Cesarea, where the citizens felt sympathetic toward the boys but dared not speak up. Only one man, an old soldier friend of Herod's named Tero, was bold enough to tell Herod how wrong it would be to kill his sons, adding that everyone in the army was sympathetic to them. Tero and everyone he mentioned in his plea, including 300 army officers, were denounced by others and put to death. Alexander and Aristobulus were promptly taken to Sebaste and strangled to death.

The boys were not totally free of blame in this whole affair, having been vain, suspicious, and disrespectful of their father for so long. Yet neither could Herod be excused for killing them without proof they were plotting against him. Certainly he could have kept them alive in bonds or banished them; as it was, his killing them out of suspicion and anger was a demonstration of great impiety.

Herod's Wives and Children

Even though Antipater's plots had succeeded in eliminating his brothers, it would be difficult for him to rule Judea, since its citizens hated him for Alexander's and Aristobulus's deaths. Even the soldiers, on whom kings depend for their safety, were alienated from him.

However, he was now jointly governing with his father, trusted by Herod and depended upon because of his loyalty, which he had demonstrated by betraying his brothers. In fact, Antipater was determined to do away with Herod and take over the kingdom, since he was afraid Herod would eventually learn the truth about him.

To obtain some badly needed friends for himself, Antipater began bestowing gifts on Herod's friends, his friends in Rome, and expecially Saturninus, the president of Syria. He tried the same tactic with Salome, but she was a woman not easily fooled, and she had known Antipater too long to be bought.

Herod was bringing up Alexander's and Aristobulus's children with great care. Alexander and Glaphyra had had two sons; Aristobulus and Bernice had had three sons and two daughters. Because the children were now fatherless, and hoping to make Antipater feel more kindly toward them by marrying them into his family, Herod arranged to have them engaged, although they were too young to marry yet. Unfortunately, Antipater hated and feared his brothers' children as much as he had hated and feared his brothers.

At this time, Herod had nine wives. One was Antipater's mother, another was the high priest's daughter, by whom he had a son named Herod. He was also married to his brother's daughter and his sister's daughter; he had no children by these wives. He had a Samaritan wife, by whom he had three children: Antipas, Archelaus, and Olympias. Olympias was later married to Joseph, Herod's brother's son. Archelaus and Antipas were being brought up by a private citizen in Rome. Cleopatra of Jerusalem gave Herod two sons, Herod and Philip. Philip was also growing up in Rome. Another wife, Pallas, gave him a son named Phasaelus. Besides these, he was married to Phedra and Elpia, who had given him daughters named Roxana and Salome. His two eldest daughters by Mariamne, whom Pheroras had refused to marry, were married to Salome's son Antipater and Phaselaus, his brother's son.

Zamaris

To secure his territory from the attacks of the Trachonite robbers, Herod decided to build a city near Trachonitis, populate it with Jews, and use it as a base for fighting the robbers. When he heard of a Babylonian Jew named Zamaris who was living at Antioch by Daphne of Syria, he sent for him. This man already had five hundred of his own horsemen, all accomplished archers, plus a family of over one hundred. The Babylonian was convinced to take possession of some land next to Trachonitis, where he built a fortress and village named Bathyra, protected the area, and safeguarded all the Jews going between Babylon and Jerusalem to offer sacrifices. In return for his protection, no tax or tribute was collected from Bathyra, which was soon populated by Jewish citizens looking for safety and freedom from taxation.

The Women

All the public affairs of the kingdom now depended on Antipater. He could reward whomever he pleased and was formidable to all, not so much because of his authority as of his shrewdness in eliminating his brothers. His best friend soon became Pheroras, Herod's brother.

Soon Pheroras's wife, and her mother and sister, and Doris, Antipater's mother, all became close friends. They kept their friendship secret because they were afraid Herod would think they were plotting against him, but Salome found out about it and carried the news to Herod, warning him the women could be up to no good.

While Herod was worried, there was nothing he could do about this group of women, since they were friendly with the Pharisees. The Pharisees, who had a history of opposing kings, were a cunning and powerful sect. When all the Jews had been forced to swear allegiance to Caesar and Herod, the Pharisees — over 6,000 strong — had refused, and their fine had been paid by Pheroras's wife. To pay her back, the Pharisees, who were believed to have foreknowledge of things by divine inspiration, prophesied that Herod's government would cease and his children would never rule; the kingdom would fall to Pheroras and his mother.

Salome, who always knew everything, heard of it, and news of the prophecy and of the Pharisees' influence in the palace came to Herod's ears, with the result that Herod executed those Pharisees implicated in giving the prophecy.

After Herod punished the Pharisees, he gathered together an assembly of his friends and accused Pheroras's wife of starting a quarrel between himself and Pheroras and being responsible for the general uproar within the palace, adding that Pheroras would do well to divorce her.

Pheroras, who had once turned down Herod's offer of his two eldest daughters in favor of his wife, refused, stating that he could no more stop loving his wife than he could stop loving his brother, Herod. At this point Herod backed down, although he did command Antipater and his mother, Doris, to stay away from the group of women in Pheroras's family. They promised to do so, but continued to meet with them. It is also reported that Antipater had sexual relations with Pheroras's wife at the urging of his mother.

Antipater began to worry that he was falling out of favor

with Herod. To get away from the palace for a while, he arranged to be called to Rome by Caesar. Herod allowed him to go, sending his will to Caesar at the same time. According to the will, Antipater was to succeed Herod; second in line was Herod Philip, Herod's son by the high priest's daughter.

As to Pheroras, Herod informed him that if he was so in love with his wife, he should go live with her in his own tetrarchy, which Pheroras did gladly, swearing he would not return until Herod was dead. True to his word, Pheroras refused to return to Herod when Herod became ill and asked for him. But when Pheroras suddenly took ill, Herod went to him without being called. Upon Pheroras's death, Herod took care of his funeral, bringing him to Jerusalem to be buried.

THREE

Soon after Pheroras's funeral, two of his freedmen came to Herod and asked that he investigate the death, for they believed Pheroras had been poisoned by his wife. Using his normal approach to obtain the truth, Herod began torturing slaves, one of whom laid the blame on Antipater's mother. In time, he learned the facts.

The first information to emerge concerned Antipater's feelings for his father, whom he believed was living far too long. Antipater also resented the fact that if he were to die before inheriting the crown, it would not go to his sons, but to his brother Herod Philip. These confessions agreed with what Salome had been telling Herod all along. Because he felt she had acted out of spite, Herod promptly took away Doris's jewels and sent her away.

More information came to light when Antipater's procurator was tortured. According to him, Antipater had prepared a poison and given it to Pheroras, telling him to kill Herod while Antipater was safely in Rome. Pheroras was said to have entrusted the potion to his wife.

Hoping to avoid torture, Pheroras's wife tried to kill herself. She failed, then promptly told Herod all she knew. Pheroras had accepted the potion and turned it over to her, but when he fell sick and Herod treated him so kindly, Pheroras ordered his wife to burn the potion in his sight. She had, only reserving a little of it to use on herself, if necessary. She produced the remaining poison for Herod.

The high priest's daughter, one of Herod's wives, had known of the plot without warning Herod. He divorced her and disinherited her son, Herod Philip, who was second in line behind Antipater. He also took the high priesthood away from her father, Simon, and gave it to Matthias, the son of Theophilus.

While all this was going on, Bathyllus, Antipater's freedman, arrived from Rome carrying a second poisoned potion that he was to give to Antipater's mother and Pheroras's mother, in case the first poison didn't work. Soon letters arrived from Antipater accusing Archelaus and Philip, who were living in Rome, of being angry at Herod for killing their brothers. Antipater was still plotting away, even though he had been exposed for seven months. As far as he knew, nothing had gone wrong. All the roads were being carefully guarded to prevent any messages from reaching him, and no one liked him enough to risk his life for him.

Antipater wrote that he was coming home; Herod replied affectionately to assure Antipater that he suspected nothing, then arranged to have Quintilius Varus, the new president of Syria, present to judge Antipater when he arrived. Upon reaching the castle, Antipater was admitted, but his friends were not.

Antipater was brought before Varus and Herod the following day. Herod bewailed the actions of his son, and when he could speak no more, Nicolaus served as Herod's prosecutor. When Nicolaus had laid out the entire case against Antipater, Varus encouraged him to present his defense, but all Antipater could manage to do was appeal to God, asking Him to testify to his innocence. Varus called for the potion to satisfy himself that it was indeed poisoned, which he proved by administering it to a condemned person, who promptly died. Antipater was imprisoned, and Varus left for home the next day, no one knowing what he and Herod had decided.

Herod sent letters and witnesses to Caesar and waited for permission to kill his son.

Herod's Illness

As his ambassadors made their way to Caesar, Herod fell ill and redrew his will, leaving the kingdom to his youngest son, Antipas. Herod was now about seventy years old, convinced he was dying unloved by either his family or his subjects.

Hearing the hated king was dying, two well-respected Jewish educators, Judas and Matthias, urged their students to pull down the golden eagle Herod had erected over the temple gate in defiance of the Jewish law about images. They warned the students they would probably die in the attempt, but that it would be a worthy and long-remembered death.

In the middle of the day, in front of the crowd in the temple, the students climbed the temple gate, pulled down the golden eagle, and cut it to pieces with axes. The king's captain and his soldiers attacked the students, capturing forty of them with Judas and Matthias, and brought them to Herod. Since they were unrepentant, Herod had them bound and sent to Jericho. Calling together the Jewish leaders at Jericho, Herod, now too sick to stand, told them that what the students had done was sacrilege. He also mentioned all his own good works, including the building of the temple. The Jewish leaders agreed the students should be punished, and all forty were burned alive with their two teachers. At the same time, Herod removed the high priest from office and replaced him. That night (March 13, 4 B.C.) there was an eclipse of the moon.

By now Herod was deathly ill; some said in punishment for his impiety. He was continuously hungry, suffering from a high fever, had extreme pains in his lower abdomen, difficulty in breathing, and convulsions. Having no hopes of recovering, he ordered every soldier paid fifty drachmae and gave his friends large sums of money.

Returning to Jericho, he called the leaders of the entire Jewish nation to him. Since refusal meant death, most of them came. Herod had them all locked up in the hippodrome, called

Salome and her husband, Alexas, to him, and instructed them to kill everyone in the hippodrome as soon as he died. They were also to put to death one member of every family in the kingdom. The mourning such a massacre would cause would also serve as mourning for Herod — something his death by itself would certainly not cause among the Jews.

Antipater's Death

As Herod was giving these orders to his family, letters arrived from his ambassadors in Rome giving Caesar's permission for Herod to deal with Antipater as he saw fit. Herod called for an apple and knife, then suddenly tried to kill himself with the knife. His first cousin, Achiabus, prevented him from doing so and called for help.

Hearing the uproar, Antipater assumed Herod was dead and demanded to be set free to take over the throne, but his jailer refused, reporting Antipater's demands to Herod; Herod ordered Antipater's immediate execution and dishonorable burial in Hyrcania.

Herod's Death

Before he died, Herod amended his will again, appointing Antipas tetrarch of Galilee and Berea and giving the kingdom to his son Archelaus. Philip received Gaulonitis, Trachonitis, and Paneas. Salome received 500,000 silver drachmae, Jamnia, Ashdod, and Phasaelis. All other family members were left cash and yearly revenues. Caesar received 10 million drachmae; Julia, Caesar's wife, received vessels of gold and silver and costly garments.

Five days after Antipater's death, Herod died (4 B.C.), having reigned thirty-four years from the time of Antigonus's death. He was a man of great barbarity and a slave of his passions, above any consideration of right and wrong, yet he was as favored by fortune as any man ever was, a private man who became king. Surrounded by dangers, he lived to an old age and thought himself fortunate in his family and children because he could always conquer his enemies among them.

Before Herod's death was announced, Salome and Alexas released the Jewish leaders being held in the hippodrome and sent them home, instead of having them killed. Herod's will was read before the soldiers in the hippodrome, who acclaimed Archelaus king, although the title would not legally be his until the will was approved by Caesar. Archelaus made the arrangements for Herod's funeral.

Herod's body was carried on a golden bier embroidered with precious stones; both the bier and the body were covered with purple. Herod was adorned with a diadem and crown of gold, a sceptre in his right hand. His sons and relatives stood around the bier, followed by the soldiery: first his guards, then bands of Thracians, Germans, and Galatians. Behind these marched the whole army in battle order. Five hundred of Herod's domestics followed, carrying spices. The procession traveled to Herodium, where Herod was buried.

Archelaus mourned for the seven days appointed by Jewish law, then went to the temple amid acclamations from the people, where he ascended a golden throne and spoke. He thanked the people for receiving him as their king, but would not accept the title of king until it was properly given to him by Caesar. Nevertheless, he did much that the crowd requested, freeing Herod's prisoners and relieving the people of some of their taxes. Following this, he offered sacrifices at the temple and went off to feast with his friends.

Sedition

As Archelaus prepared to go to Rome to see if Caesar would confirm him as king of Judea, sedition broke out among some of the Jews who were sympathetic to the teachers and students killed by Herod, believing they had not been properly mourned. With much uproar and lamentation, they cast blame on Archelaus as well as his father, as though that would help the deceased students. A group gathered together to demand that Archelaus punish those who had been honored by Herod for the students' deaths. Their main demand, which Archelaus granted, was that he choose a new high priest, one purer and more acceptable to Jewish law.

Archelaus sent his general to talk to the people, instructing him to remind them the students' deaths had been in accordance with the law. He also told the general to request that they wait until Caesar gave the government to Archelaus, at which time he could legally discuss their petitions with them. Until then, they should keep quiet, lest they seem seditious.

The crowd refused to listen to the general or to anyone else Archelaus sent to reason with them, feeling so strongly about their demands that they didn't worry about their personal safety. It was insufferable to them that having lost those most dear to them under Herod, they could not get the guilty parties punished by Archelaus. The crowd, which was growing larger every day, refused all Archelaus's ambassadors, treating them as private citizens and refusing to let them speak.

Passover was approaching; Jerusalem was filling with Jews from all Judea and beyond, coming to offer their sacrifices at the temple, where the seditious crowd was staying. Afraid that all the pilgrims would be aroused by the group in the temple, Archelaus sent a regiment of soldiers to suppress the uproar and bring any troublemakers to him. The protesters incited the crowd to attack the soldiers, stoning them until they retreated.

Archelaus was now sure the government would be overthrown unless the protesters were stopped; he sent the whole army in to restore order. The horsemen were ordered to prevent anyone outside the temple from aiding those inside and to track down anyone escaping from the foot soldiers. Three thousand people were killed; the rest of the crowd fled to the hills. Ordering everyone to return home, Archelaus left for Rome.

Archelaus Before Caesar

Archelaus went to his ship with his mother, Nicolaus, Ptolemy, and many of his friends, leaving his brother Philip in charge at home. Salome and her family also went, supposedly to assist Archelaus in gaining his crown. Secretly, they intended to oppose him, complain of his actions at the temple, and have Antipas declared king.

At the same time, Sabinus, Caesar's steward for Syrian affairs, was traveling to Judea to safeguard Herod's estate until his will was approved by Caesar. He and Archelaus met at Cesarea with Varus, the president of Syria. Sabinus promised Varus that he would not seize any of Herod's property until Caesar made his decision. However, as soon as Archelaus left for Rome and Varus for Antioch, Sabinus promptly went to Jerusalem and seized the king's palace. He sent for the keepers of the garrisons and those in charge of Herod's effects and warned them he expected them to give an account of what they had. Those who had been left in charge of Herod's possessions continued to follow Archelaus's instructions, telling Sabinus they were keeping the property safe for Caesar.

Another of Herod's sons, Antipas, was also on the way to Rome, hoping to gain the throne with Salome's help. When Antipas reached Rome, the family all turned to support his claim. Although they would have preferred independence under a Roman governor, if there had to be a king, they wanted it to be Antipas. Sabinus also sent letters to Caesar against Archelaus.

Archelaus, believing the throne was his, sent his papers to Caesar: letters substantiating his claim, Herod's will, an account of Herod's possessions, and Herod's seal. Caesar read these papers, along with the letters from Varus and Sabinus containing a summary of Herod's estate and yearly revenues, and knowing Antipas was also claiming the kingdom, called everyone together.

The first to speak was Salome's son, Antipater, a gifted orator and enemy of Archelaus. He claimed Archelaus had already seized power without Caesar's approval, punishing those in the temple without authority and thereby depriving Caesar of his rights. In addition, Archelaus had changed the commanders in the army, occupied the royal throne, judged lawsuits, and behaved improperly by partying with his friends during mourning for his father. Antipater's main charge concerned the temple massacre, which he called impiety leading to the death of some foreigners and other innocent people. He also added that Herod had not been in his right mind when he changed his will in Archelaus's favor.

Next to speak was Nicolaus, who took the side of Archelaus. He blamed the temple deaths on the Jewish troublemakers who forced Archelaus to use arms to keep the peace and maintain the authority of Caesar. As to the will, Nicolaus maintained Herod's mind was sound when it was drawn up, but was not when the one favoring Antipas was made. He appealed to Caesar, as Herod's old friend, not to betray his friendship and trust now that Herod was gone.

Caesar assured Archelaus he would not violate Herod's will, but did not confirm him as king at that assembly. Instead he gave himself time to decide whether to confirm Archelaus or split the kingdom up among Herod's heirs.

Rebellion

Before Caesar's decision was made, Mathace, Archelaus's mother, fell sick and died. Letters also arrived from Varus, telling Caesar that the whole country had fallen into tumult and rebellion as soon as Archelaus left for Rome. Since he was there, Varus had punished the leaders of the disturbance and left a legion of his army behind in Jerusalem when he returned home, but Sabinus had used these forces so brutally in collecting Herod's riches that the whole nation had rebelled against him.

When the festival of Pentecost arrived, many tens of thousands of men flowed into the city, not only to celebrate, but out of indignation at Sabinus. There were people from Galilee, Idumea, Jericho, and other lands over the Jordan. All joined together, divided themselves into three bands, and encamped. One group seized the hippodrome; one took over the temple; the third occupied the section of Jerusalem containing the palace. They had the one Roman legion completely surrounded.

Sabinus sent to Varus for help, barricaded himself in the fortress named Phasaelus, and ordered the legion to attack the crowd at the temple. The soldiers killed a great many of the crowd, but had problems with some of them who climbed to the top of the cloisters to throw down rocks and use their bows. These men were out of range of the Roman archers because the cloisters were so tall, so the Romans set the cloisters on fire. A number of people were killed when the roof collapsed; others threw themselves into the fire or fell on their own swords. Those who climbed down were all killed, although they were unarmed.

After all the crowd in the temple was killed, the soldiers looted the temple treasury. Sabinus himself took 400 talents.

Those still left in the rebellion surrounded the palace, threatening to set it on fire and kill everyone inside. Before they did anything, they ordered everyone out of the castle, promising they would not be harmed. The greatest part of Herod's troops surrendered, but Rufus and Gratus, who had 3,000 of Herod's troops and a band of horsemen under them, went over to the Romans.

The Jews kept up the siege of the palace, mining under the walls and asking those who had gone over to the Romans not to hinder them now that there was an opportunity to restore their country's freedom.

Rebellions were breaking out all over Judea. Two thousand of Herod's former soldiers, who had previously been disbanded, got together again to fight the king's troops. Achiabus, Herod's first cousin, fought them but was driven into the mountains.

There was also a man named named Judas, son of Ezekias, the head of the robbers whom Herod had captured with great difficulty. He gathered a group of men together near Sepphoris in Galilee, assaulted the palace there, armed his men with weapons from the palace, and took away the money stored there. He was purposefully vicious with everyone he encountered, hoping to build a reputation for himself.

Simon, one of Herod's slaves who had proved superior to other slaves and been trusted with many duties, burned down and plundered the palace in Jericho, along with many of the king's other houses all over the country. Gratus, who had gone over to the Romans, destroyed Simon's forces after a long battle; Simon was captured as he attempted to escape and was beheaded.

Because there was no king to keep order, the whole country

was in turmoil. No small part of the blame must go to the foreigners who came in to keep the peace, since their greed and brutality only made things unbearable.

A man named Athronges proclaimed himself king, although he was really no more than a shepherd. He and his four brothers, all with unusual strength in their hands and uncommonly tall, ruled over their own large bands of men. These men killed many of the Romans and the king's men, hating them all. Herod's soldiers were despised because of their licentious conduct under Herod; the Romans because of their recent attacks on the Jews. They once attacked a company of Romans at Emmaus who were bringing wheat and weapons to the army, killing the centurion Arius and forty of his best foot soldiers. These men continued warring against all sides for a long period.

Each group of robbers that was formed proclaimed its own leader a king and, in some measure, hurt the Romans, but the citizens of the area suffered the most.

Varus's Army

As soon as Varus received Sabinus's letter, he took his two remaining legions, four troops of horsemen, and other forces that were lent to him, and hurried toward Judea. The citizens of Berytus gave him fifteen hundred auxiliaries as he passed through their city. Aretas sent him assistance. Some of his forces were sent to Galilee, where they took back Sepphoris, enslaved the citizens, and burned the city. Varus himself continued on to Samaria, which he left alone because it had not joined the seditions. He traveled through Arus, Sampho, and Emmaus, plundering and burning any town in rebellion. When he arrived in Jerusalem, some of the besieging Jews left rather than fight his army, and the palace siege was broken.

The Jerusalem Jews denied being part of the rebellion, claiming that the crowds had all come for the feast and been stirred up by foreigners, not natives. Varus was met by Joseph (Herod's cousin), Gratus, Rufus, and the Romans who had been besieged; Sabinus sneaked out of the city and made his way to the sea without seeing Varus.

Varus sent his forces out into the country to capture those responsible for the revolt; 2,000 people were crucified for their actions. Finding his troops becoming impossible to control, Varus dismissed them. Ten thousand Jews surrendered to Varus on Achiabus's advice; he dismissed all but their commanders, whom he sent to Caesar. Caesar dismissed the charges against all of them except those related to Herod; those he punished for fighting against their own family.

The Jewish Ambassadors

Once Varus had restored order, he returned to Antioch, but before he left, he gave the Jews permission to send ambassadors to Rome to petition for freedom to live under their own laws. Fifty ambassadors traveled to Rome, where they joined the more than 8,000 Jews already living there.

Caesar assembled his friends and high-ranking Romans in the temple of Apollo to receive the ambassadors along with Archelaus and his friends. Those in Archelaus's family who opposed him did not attend to support him, but neither did they appear to assist the ambassadors. Philip arrived at the urging of Varus, to help his brother.

The Jewish ambassadors accused Herod of being a tyrant, persecuting them, and taking away their estates. While he built and adorned cities populated by foreigners, his kingdom's cities were destroyed, until his once prosperous land was now filled with poverty. They also complained not only of unjust taxation, but of the necessity of bribing Herod's friends to avoid unjust violence. Although they had suffered much before in their history, nothing compared to their suffering under Herod. At first, they claimed, they had welcomed Archelaus as their new king; then he had shown his true nature by killing 3,000 people in the temple.

They petitioned Caesar to abolish the royal government of Judea and join the country to Syria, to be ruled by Roman presidents.

Nicolaus spoke in Herod's defense, saying Herod had never been accused this way during his lifetime (which was not true),

51

so why should he be accused in death? Archelaus's actions he defended as necessary to maintain justice and the laws.

Caesar Divides Herod's Estate

A few days after this assembly, Caesar appointed Archelaus ethnarch of half of Herod's kingdom, promising to treat him as a king if he governed virtuously. The other half was divided into two parts, Philip and Antipas each ruling one part. Antipas was to receive the yearly tribute of 200 talents from Perea and Galilee. Batanea, Trachonitis, Auranitis, and part of the house of Lenodorus would pay tribute of 100 talents to Philip. Idumea, Judea, and Samaria paid tribute to Archelaus, but Caesar relieved them of one-quarter of that amount because they had not joined the revolt. Other cities would pay Archelaus: Strato's Tower, Sebaste, Joppa, and Jerusalem. Gaza, Gadara, and Hippos, which were Grecian cities, were added to the province of Syria. In total, Archelaus would collect 600 talents (45,000 pounds of silver) a year.

Salome also did very well. Herod had left her Jamnia, Ashdod, Phasaelis, and 500,000 drachmae of coined silver. To this, Caesar added a palace in Askelon. In all, her revenues amounted to 60 talents a year (4,500 pounds); her dwelling was within Archelaus's territory. The rest of Herod's relatives received whatever his will stipulated. Caesar made a gift of 250,000 silver drachmae to Herod's two eldest daughters and married them to Pheroras's sons. Everything Herod had left to Caesar, except a few of the vessels he kept as a remembrance, was divided among Herod's sons — a total of 1,500 talents (112,500 pounds).

FOUR

There was at this time a young Jew who had been raised by a Roman freedman in the city of Sidon. The young man bore a remarkable resemblance to Alexander, the son Herod had killed some years ago, and when people began to notice the resemblance, he decided to use his appearance to obtain some money and power for himself.

He hired an assistant from Sidon, a man well acquainted with the affairs of the palace who was skilled in influencing the public and willing to teach the boy his skills. Then he declared himself to be Alexander, Herod's son, saying he had been saved by one of the men ordered to kill him and had been hidden away with his brother, Aristobulus.

Traveling to Crete, he convinced all the Jews who came to see him that he was Alexander and received substantial amounts of money from them. He moved on to Melos, collecting even more money and support from those he fooled, who hoped to profit when he claimed his kingdom. Landing in Dicearchia, he fooled the Jews there, as well as all of Herod's old friends, who accepted him as their new king.

Even those who had personally known Alexander accepted the young man's claims and rejoiced in his escape from death,

53

for Mariamne's family was loved by all the Jews. Arriving in Rome, he was met by all the Jews living there, who carried him in a royal litter through the streets with all the trappings of royalty — at their own expense. Roman crowds gathered around to acclaim him; he received every honor due a returning prince.

But Caesar had doubts about the young man's claim, knowing Herod had not been an easy man to fool, especially about important matters such as his sons' execution. Yet he wasn't positive, so he sent Celadus, a freedman who had known Alexander personally, to bring the young man to him. On meeting him, even Celadus accepted the man as Alexander.

The only man he couldn't fool was Caesar, who saw the few differences that existed between him and Alexander. Alexander had been an educated, pampered prince; this man's hands were rough, his body rugged. Seeing how the man and his teacher agreed on every point, Caesar asked what had become of Aristobulus. Why hadn't he come with Alexander, so Caesar could give him his inheritance?

They replied that Aristobulus was waiting in Crete, so in case anything happened to "Alexander," at least one of them would survive. Caesar took the young man off by himself, away from his teacher, and told him he had better tell the truth if he wanted to live. He also asked who planned this story, knowing it was too well-done to be arranged by someone as young as Alexander's look-alike.

The imposter realized he had no choice but to tell the truth and admitted he was not Alexander. True to his promise, Caesar let the boy live as a ship's rower, for he was young and strong, but his adviser was executed. The people of Melos who had supported the imposter were not punished; Caesar decided their lost money was punishment enough for their foolishness.

Archelaus's Banishment

When Archelaus returned to his ethnarchy in Judea, he accused the high priest, Joazar the son of Boethus, of assisting the rebellion, took away his office, and presented it to Joazar's brother, Eleazar, who was soon to be replaced by Jesus the son of Sie.

Archelaus rebuilt the royal palace at Jericho, diverting half the village of Neara's water to water the palm tree plantation at the castle. Then he built a village he named Archelaus. Disobeying the Jewish law that forbids a man from marrying his brother's wife if she had children by her first husband, Archelaus married Glaphyra, who already had three children by Alexander.

In the tenth year of Archelaus's rule as ethnarch of Judea, the principal men of Judea and Samaria, along with Archelaus's brothers, accused him before Caesar for his barbarous behavior toward them. Caesar had warned Archelaus to rule with justice when he appointed him ethnarch, so these accusations infuriated him. Too angry to write to him, Caesar sent for Archelaus's Roman steward (also named Archelaus) and told him to go bring Archelaus to him in Rome.

Five days before his steward arrived with the summons, Archelaus dreamed of ten ears of fully ripe corn that were eaten by oxen. On waking, he sent for his diviners to learn what the dream meant. The diviners could not agree on the dream's meaning, but Simon, an Essen, asked permission to speak freely, saying the dream indicated a change in Archelaus's life — not a good change. He believed the oxen represented afflictions as well as a change in affairs, since land that is ploughed by oxen is changed land. The ten ears of corn represented ten years, since an ear of corn takes a whole season to grow. The Essen predicted that Archelaus's reign was about to end.

Archelaus was not the only member of his family to suffer from dreams; his wife, Glaphyra, also had one. After Alexander's death, she had married Juba, the king of Libya. Upon his death, she lived as a widow with her father in his kingdom of Cappadocia until Archelaus divorced his wife, Mariamne, and married her. During her marriage to Archelaus, she saw her first husband, Alexander, in a dream. She embraced him with joy until he reproved her for her remarriages, especially for the unlawful one to his brother. In the dream, Alexander said he would not hold her remarriages against her but would cause her to be his again; a few days after telling her women friends about the dream, Glaphyra died.

When Archelaus arrived in Rome as summoned, Caesar banished him to Vienna and took away his money. His country was merged with the province of Syria, and Cyrenius was sent to sell the house of Archelaus.

The Jewish Sects

Cyrenius, a Roman senator and consul, arrived in Syria to serve as a judge and make an accounting of Syrian possessions, as well as dispose of Archelaus's estate. Coponius was sent with him to govern the Jews, who were now living as part of the Syrian province.

At first the Jews protested the new taxation, but the high priest, Joazar the son of Boethus, quieted them and they peacefully gave accountings of their estates to Cyrenius.

But one man, Judas, who was from Gamala in Galilee, encouraged the people to rebel against the taxation. Together with Sadduc, a Pharisee, he told the people this taxation was the beginning of their slavery, exhorting them to assert their freedom and promising them happiness, security, and God's blessings for their bold actions. Rebellions and wars broke out, killing a great number of people, including many Jewish leaders. At the same time, famine struck, cities were taken, and the temple was burned.

Judas and Sadduc formed a fourth philosophical sect among the Jews, one with a large number of followers among the younger generation. Agreeing largely with the Pharisees in most matters, this sect had a firm commitment to personal liberty, claiming that God was their only ruler and lord. Not fearing their own deaths or those of their families, they refused to call any man lord and showed willingness to undergo any amount of pain for their beliefs.

The Pharisees lived a simple life guided by reason. They respected and obeyed the guidance of their elders, and although they believed fate determined all things, they granted men freedom to act and think as they saw fit, believing God's will was accomplished through individual personalities. Pharisees believed in the soul's survival and its reward or punishment after death, with the bad man's soul undergoing eternal imprisonment and the good man's living again. Because of the popularity of their doctrines and their good example, the Pharisees controlled Jewish religious life.

The Sadducees were another Jewish sect of this period. They believed that souls die with bodies and strictly followed the Jewish law. Few followed this sect, but those who did were highly regarded. When reluctantly appointed magistrates, as they sometimes were, Sadducees tended to adopt the rules of the Pharisees that were supported by the people.

The Essens believed that all things come from God. They taught the immortality of the soul and the rewards of righteous living. Although they sent offerings to the temple, Essens refrained from sacrificing there, preferring to do that on their own, which caused them to be excluded from the common court of the temple. Since they were devoted to husbandry, their lives were more prosperous than the lives of others, and they were considered far more virtuous and righteous than any other men had ever been.

All Essen property was held in common; none were either rich or poor. About 4,000 men were Essens at this time. Neither marrying nor keeping servants, they lived by themselves and ministered to one another. Righteous men and priests were appointed to act as stewards of their revenues, and although these men controlled vast sums of money, they lived the same lives as their brothers, resembling those Dacae called *polistoe* (city dwellers).

The Roman Procurators

When Cyrenius had disposed of Archelaus's money and finished the taxation (A.D. 7), he took the high priesthood away from Joazar and appointed Ananus, the son of Seth, to that position.

Herod and Philip had each received their tetrarchies and set their affairs in order. Herod built a wall around Sepphoris, to secure all of the area around Galilee, and made Sepphoris the metropolis of the country. He also walled Betharanphtha and renamed it Julias in honor of Caesar's wife.

Philip built up Paneas, at the fountains of Jordan, renaming it Cesarea, then added to the village of Bethsaida, at Lake Gennesareth, and renamed it Julias in honor of Caesar's daughter.

Coponius was now acting as the Roman procurator of Judea. One year when the feast of Passover arrived, the priests opened the temple gates just after midnight, as was customary. As soon as they were opened, some Samaritans came into Jerusalem, entered the temple, and threw dead bodies about in the cloisters. Because of this, the Samaritans were excluded from the temple and the temple was guarded much more carefully in the future.

A little after this, Coponius returned to Rome; he was replaced as procurator by Marcus Ambivius. During Ambivius's term, Salome died, leaving Caesar's wife, Julia, the towns of Jamnia, Phasaelis, and Archelaus, with its large plantation of palms.

Annius Rufus succeeded Marcus Ambivius as procurator. During his term Caesar, the second Roman emperor, died at seventy-seven after a reign of fifty-seven years, six months, and two days (fourteen of those years he ruled jointly with Antony). Tiberius became the third Roman emperor in A.D. 14.

Tiberius sent Valerius Gratus to succeed Rufus as procurator of Judea. Gratus deposed Ananus from the high priesthood and installed Ismael, the son of Phabi, who was soon replaced by Eleazar, the son of Ananus. Eleazar held the office for one year before Gratus deprived him of it and awarded it to Simon, the son of Camithus; Simon lost the office in one year to Joseph Caiaphas. After serving in Judea for eleven years, Gratus was replaced by Pontius Pilate.

The Eastern Kingdoms

Herod the tetrarch was in great favor with Tiberius, for whom he named a new city at Lake Gennesareth. Herod populated Tiberius with foreigners, Galileans, and others he forced to move into the city from surrounding lands, as well as with poor people he collected from all parts of his tetrarchy. Some of these people were slaves whom Herod set free on the condition that they remain in Tiberius. He built all these people fine houses and gave them land, well aware that building Tiberius was a transgression of ancient Jewish law, since many sepulchres were removed to build the city.

About this time Phraates, king of the Parthians, died. While he had legitimate sons, Phraates also had an Italian maid named Thermusa, whom Caesar had sent to him as a gift. At first she was only his concubine, but Phraates was so taken with her beauty that he made her his legitimate wife and had a son by her named Phraataces.

Thermusa wanted her son to succeed Phraates, but she knew that would not happen unless his legitimate sons left the country, so she persuaded Phraates to send his two sons to Rome as pledges of his loyalty.

Even though he was now the sole heir to the throne, Phraataces grew tired of waiting to inherit. He and his mother plotted against Phraates and arranged his death. It was also said that Phraataces had sexual relations with his mother. His parricide and immorality caused Phraataces to be hated so much by his subjects that they expelled him; he died in exile.

The law of the Parthians required that their king be from the family of Arsaces, so Orodes was called to become king. He was a man accused of great cruelty and violent temper, but he was an Arsaces. Orodes was murdered; some say during a festival, others say while hunting. The Parthians then sent ambassadors to Rome to ask that one of Phraate's sons be appointed king and allowed to return. Caesar agreed, sending them Vonones.

However, the barbarians soon changed their minds, deciding Vonones, although he was Phraates's son, had been made unworthy by being sent as a virtual slave to Rome. They invited Artabanus, king of Media (and an Arsaces), to be king. He accepted, arriving with his army only to be met by Vonones, who defeated him in battle and sent him retreating to Media. Artabanus rebuilt his army, returned, and this time defeated Vonones, who escaped on horseback to Selucia on the Tigris.

Eventually Vonones fled to Armenia, which he decided he would like to rule. Tiberius refused to give it to him, so Vonones surrendered to Silanus, the president of Syria, who allowed him to remain in his country. Armenia was given to Orodes, one of Artabanus's sons.

At this time Antiochus, king of Commagene, died. That country's multitude wanted to be ruled by kings, as was traditional, but its nobility preferred the country be made a Roman province. Both sides sent ambassadors to Rome to plead their cases. The Roman senate decreed that Germanicus should go settle the affairs of the east, which he did before he was poisoned by Piso.

Pilate and the Jews

Pontius Pilate, the procurator of Judea, moved his army from Cesarea to winter quarters in Jerusalem, where he planned to abolish the Jewish laws. Former procurators had always had their armies enter the city accompanied by flags carrying no pictures of men, out of respect for the Jewish laws forbidding images, but Pilate's flags bearing Caesar's likeness were secretly erected throughout Jerusalem during the night.

As soon as the flags were discovered, crowds of Jews traveled to Cesarea to demand Pilate remove them. He refused, feeling it would be a dishonor to Caesar if he were to comply with the Jews and take the flags down. The crowd continued to petition Pilate for five days. On the sixth day, Pilate concealed soldiers in the area of his judgment seat, and when the crowd came to petition him again, they were surrounded and threatened with immediate death unless they abandoned their cause and returned home. The Jews threw themselves to the ground, bared their necks to the soldiers' weapons, and said they would willingly die before abandoning their laws. Pilate, impressed by their determination and courage, ordered the flags returned to Cesarea.

Deciding Jerusalem was in need of more water, Pilate planned to bring in a stream from a source of water twenty-five miles away. To finance the work, he used sacred money from the temple, again angering the Jews. Thousands of them gathered to insist he abandon his plan, some of them openly reproaching and talking against Pilate, as crowds are apt to do.

Pilate dressed a great number of soldiers in the same manner as the crowd was dressed, then had them hide their weapons under their clothing and secretly surround the protesters. When he told them to disperse to their homes and they began to boldly reproach him, Pilate signaled his soldiers, who attacked the crowd more viciously than Pilate had ordered, killing many of the peaceful as well as the unruly.

There was about this time a wise man named Jesus — if it is lawful to call him a man, for he was a doer of wonderful works — a teacher of the type of men who enjoy hearing the truth. He drew many of the Jews and Gentiles to him; he was the Christ. When Pilate, at the suggestion of the Jewish leaders, condemned him to the cross, those that loved him at first did not forsake him, for he appeared to them alive the third day, as the divine prophets had foretold, along with many other wonderful things concerning him. The tribe of Christians named for him still exists today.

The Banishment of the Jews

Living in Rome at this time was a Jew who had fled his own country when accused of transgressing Jewish law. He and three equally wicked men persuaded Fulvia, a prominent Roman woman who had converted to Judaism, to send purple cloth and gold to the temple as an offering. They accepted the money from her to buy the offering and promptly spent it all on themselves.

Fulvia's husband, Saturninus, asked Tiberius to see what had become of his wife's donation. When Tiberius discovered its theft by the four Jews, he ordered the banishment of all Jews from the city of Rome. Four thousand Jews were sent to the island of Sardinia, while a great number of them were killed for refusing to become soldiers, which they said was forbidden by their law. Thus the wickedness of four men resulted in the banishment of all the Jews from Rome.

The Samaritans

The Samaritan Jews were also having problems with the Romans. One Samaritan Jew urged the others to join him on Mount Gerizzim, which was considered a holy mountain, promising to show them sacred vessels that had supposedly been hidden there by Moses. An armed crowd that believed the man's story gathered at a village named Tirathaba near the mountain, planning to go up the mountain together.

Pilate prevented the crowd from climbing the mountain by sending soldiers to take control of the roads and turn the crowd back. That done, the soldiers then attacked the village itself, slaying some Jews and taking many prisoner; the crowd's leaders were put to death by Pilate.

The Samaritan senate sent an ambassador to Vitellius, the president of Syria, accusing Pilate of murdering the Jews in the village, who were not revolting, but trying to escape Pilate's rampaging soldiers on the roads. Vitellius sent Marcellus, a personal friend of his, to manage Judea and ordered Pilate to Rome to answer the Samaritan charges before Caesar. Pilate had been procurator of Judea for ten years before he returned to Rome.

Vitellius

Vitellius himself arrived in Jerusalem during Passover and was warmly received by the Jews there. While there, he released the country from the tax levied on fruits that were bought or sold and gave the temple priests permission to care for the high priest's vestments and ornaments, instead of having them locked in the tower of Antonia and guarded by the Romans.

Many years ago, the first high priest of the Jews, Hyrcanus, had built himself a tower next to the temple. He lived and stored his vestments there, as did the high priests who followed him. When Herod the Great refortified the tower and named it

Antonia, he found the vestments and kept them in his own care as a way of controlling the Jews. When the Romans took over the government of Judea after Archelaus was banished, they locked the vestments in a stone chamber under the seal of the temple priests. Seven days before Passover, Pentecost, the Feast of the Tabernacles, and the Day of Atonement, the captain of the Roman guard would deliver the vestments to the high priest, who would purify them, use them for the festival, then return them to the chamber the day after the service.

Vitellius returned the care of these vestments to the Jews, relieving the captain of the guard of responsibility for their protection. He also replaced the high priest, Joseph Caiaphas, with Jonathan, the son of Ananus (a former high priest), before he returned to Antioch.

War With the Parthians

Tiberius commanded Vitellius to make a treaty with Artabanus, the king of Parthia, who had just taken over Armenia. He hoped to keep Artabanus from taking any more territory, so he told Vitellius that part of the agreement must involve hostages from Artabanus — preferably his son, also named Artabanus.

Vitellius offered the kings of Iberia and Albania a bribe to fight Artabanus for him, and although they wouldn't do the actual fighting, they allowed the Scythians to pass through their countries on their way to Parthia. Armenia was taken back from the Parthians, their leaders were slain, and the whole country fell into disorder. Artabanus's son died in the war along with many other Parthian soldiers.

Vitellius also bribed Artabanus's family to arrange his murder. Learning of the plot, Artabanus decided that too many people were against him and escaped to the upper provinces of his country, where he raised an army from the Dahae and Sacae, then returned to reclaim his kingdom.

Once more Tiberius instructed Vitellius to arrange a treaty. Vitellius and Artabanus met on a bridge over the Euphrates River and agreed to peace terms; Herod the tetrarch then erected a great tent on the bridge and entertained both men. Not long afterward, Artabanus sent his son Darius to Rome as a hostage, along with many gifts for Tiberius, one of which was a giant Jew named Eleazar, who was ten and one-half feet tall.

Herod the tetrarch, hoping to be the first with the good news, sent letters to Tiberius describing the meeting and its results in great detail. When Tiberius later received Vitellius's report, he replied he already knew everything from Herod's letters, which angered Vitellius and made him seek revenge against Herod when the chance came later.

Herod Fights Aretas

Many years before, Herod Antipas the tetrarch had married the daughter of Aretas, the king of Arabia Petrea. Now, on a visit to Rome, he stayed with his half-brother, Herod Philip, who was the son of the high priest Simon's daughter. While there, Herod Antipas fell in love with Herodias, who was Herod Philip's wife, the daughter of Aristobulus (the half-brother of both Herods), and the sister of Agrippa the Great. Herod Antipas talked to Herodias about divorcing her husband and marrying him, which she agreed to do when he returned home from Rome. Part of her agreement stipulated that he divorce his wife as she would divorce Herod Philip.

Herod Antipas finished his business in Rome and returned to Judea, unaware that his wife had heard of her upcoming divorce. She asked his permission to visit Macherus, a castle under her father's control on the border between the territories of Herod and Aretas. Thinking his wife knew nothing of his plans, Herod had her escorted to Macherus. Once there, she told her father of Herod's plan to divorce her and marry Herodias.

Aretas and Antipas were already quarreling over the border between them in Gamalitis; the additional insult to Aretas was enough to start a war between them, which Aretas won through treachery. Antipas wrote to Tiberius about the whole disagreement; Tiberius in turn wrote to Vitellius (the president of Syria), telling him to either kill Aretas, take him prisoner, or send him his head.

Many of the Jews believed Aretas's destruction of Antipas's army was just punishment from God for his killing John the Baptist. John had been a good man, commanding the Jews to be virtuous to one another and pious before God. He urged them all to be baptized for the remission of their sins and purification of their bodies and souls. The crowds that gathered around this John were so greatly moved by his words that Herod thought it best to kill him rather than risk any rebellion he might encourage. He had John taken as a prisoner to the castle at Macherus and killed.

On Tiberius's orders, Vitellius prepared to go to war with Aretas. His army, consisting of two legions of foot soldiers and horsemen, began to advance toward Petra, passing through Ptolemais, in Judea, on their way. As they passed through Judea, the Jewish leaders met Vitellius and asked him not to cross their land, since the Roman flags bore many images on them. Vitellius granted their request and diverted his army over the Great Plain, while he and Herod went to Jerusalem to offer sacrifices at the festival then going on.

Vitellius stayed in Jerusalem for three days, taking the high priesthood away from Jonathan and giving it to his brother Theophilus. On the fourth day, letters arrived informing Vitellius of Tiberius's death. He required the people of Jerusalem to take an oath of fidelity to Caius, the new emperor, then recalled his army and sent them home, since he no longer had the authority to go to war.

It's said that Aretas had consulted with his diviners when he heard of Vitellius's approach, and they had assured him that either Tiberius or Vitellius would die before they could invade his territory.

FIVE

Shortly before the death of Herod the Great, his grandson Agrippa (Aristobulus's son) was living in Rome, where he had been brought up with Drusus, the only son of the emperor Tiberius. Agrippa was well-liked by Antonia, a close friend of his mother, Bernice. Antonia herself was the wife of Drusus the Great (Tiberius's brother).

Agrippa was a naturally generous man, but as long as Bernice was alive, he was careful not to be overly extravagant. Once she died, however, Agrippa soon reduced himself to poverty by living too well and giving expensive gifts to Caesar's freedmen in hopes of gaining their goodwill. On Drusus's death, Tiberius refused to see any of his son's friends because seeing them made him mourn his only son's death even more. This combination of factors led Agrippa to leave his Roman creditors behind and flee to his home in Judea.

In shame over his unpayable debts and damaged reputation, Agrippa moved into a fortification at Malatha in Idumea, becoming so depressed that he began to think of killing himself. His wife, Cypros, realized what he was considering and sent a letter to Agrippa's sister, Herodias, who was now married to Herod the tetrarch, asking her to help Agrippa out of his problems. Herodias and her husband sent for Agrippa, made him a magistrate of the city of Tiberias, and allotted him a small income for his support. This arrangement did not really solve Agrippa's problems, since his income was still not enough to repay his debts and his pride was still wounded. One day at a feast in Tyre, Agrippa and Herod the tetrarch both got drunk and began arguing until Agrippa accused Herod of throwing his poverty in his face.

After this disagreement, Agrippa went to live with one of his friends from Rome who had since been appointed president of Syria. Flaccus received him kindly. He was already allowing Aristobulus, Agrippa's brother, to live with him, and although the two brothers were not friendly with each other, Flaccus cared for them both.

As the president of Syria, Flaccus was called on to mediate a boundary dispute between the Damascens and the Sidonians. The Damascens promised Agrippa a good bribe to influence Flaccus's decision, which Agrippa accepted. On learning of this, Agrippa's brother Aristobulus reported it to Flaccus, who found the report to be true and ordered Agrippa out of his house.

Agrippa's Return to Italy

Broke again, Agrippa traveled to Ptolemais, hoping to sail back to Italy. Since he didn't even have enough money to finance the passage, he asked his freedman, Marsyas, to borrow enough to get him there. Marsyas went to Peter, a freedman who formerly belonged to Bernice but had been left to Antonia on Bernice's death. Peter arranged a bond of 20,000 Attic drachmae for Agrippa, taking back 2,500 of them as payment for his services.

Once the money was in his possession, Agrippa traveled to Anthedon, procured a ship for the trip, and prepared to leave, only to be stopped by Herennius Capito, the procurator of Jamnia, who demanded payment of a 300,000-drachmae debt Agrippa owed him. Agrippa promised to repay the debt before leaving the country but sneaked off to Alexandria, where he asked Alexander, the governor of the Jews there, to lend him

200,000 drachmae. Alexander refused to lend the money to Agrippa, but he did agree to lend it to his wife, Cypros, whom he knew to be a virtuous woman and whom he admired for her faithfulness to Agrippa. Alexander gave Agrippa five talents in Alexandria and promised him the rest in Puteoli, afraid that Agrippa would spend the entire amount before reaching Italy if he gave it all to him in Alexandria. Cypros took on the debt herself and sent her husband off to Italy while she and the children returned to Judea.

Arriving in Puteoli, Agrippa sent a letter to Tiberius, telling him he was back in the country and that he would like to visit him in Capreae, where Tiberius was then living. Tiberius gave him permission to come see him and treated him kindly when he arrived. But the next day a letter arrived from Herennius Capito, telling Caesar how Agrippa had run off without paying his debt to him; Tiberius excluded Agrippa from his presence until the debt was paid.

Not at all worried by Tiberius's anger, Agrippa turned to Tiberius's sister-in-law, Antonia (mother of Germanicus and Claudius), asking her to lend him the 300,000 drachmae. Out of respect for his mother's memory and because Agrippa and her son Claudius had been educated together, Antonia loaned Agrippa the money to pay back Herennius Capito, and Agrippa regained Tiberius Caesar's friendship.

Tiberius recommended Agrippa to his grandson, Tiberius Gemellus, ordering the two to become friends and companions in their travels, but Agrippa preferred the friendship of Antonia's grandson, Caius (the son of Germanicus), who was more prominent than Tiberius Gemellus because of his father's good reputation. To finance this friendship, Agrippa borrowed 1 million drachmae from Thallus, one of Caesar's freedmen, repaid Antonia the 300,000 she had loaned him, and spent the remainder courting and winning Caius's friendship.

Eutychus

One day when Agrippa and Caius were riding together in a chariot, Agrippa mentioned that he hoped Tiberius would soon leave the government to Caius, who he believed was more worthy of it in every way. This comment was overheard by the chariot driver, a freedman of Agrippa's named Eutychus, who said nothing about it at the time. Later, when Agrippa rightly accused Eutychus of stealing clothing from him, Eutychus ran away from Agrippa, was captured, and brought before Piso, the city's governor. Asked why he had run away, Eutychus said he had information for Tiberius that concerned his safety; Piso had Eutychus bound and sent to Tiberius in Capreae for a hearing.

Tiberius was as slow in hearing Eutychus as he was in other governmental decisions; he never heard ambassadors quickly or sent out replacement governors or procurators to the provinces until the current ones had died. He was so negligent in these things that his friends once asked him why he acted so slowly. His reply was that he delayed seeing ambassadors to avoid having to see the second set of ambassadors that always followed on the heels of the first. He avoided replacing governors to ease the burden on his subjects. All governors try to get as much as they can from their provinces, and if one knows he will only be there for a short time, he tends to fleece his subjects as rapidly as possible, while a long-term governor will eventually satisfy himself and not be such a burden on his subjects. Although he was emperor for twenty-two years, during that time Tiberius only sent two procurators to Judea: Gratus and Pilate. Tiberius also said he delayed in hearing prisoners because they suffered while they waited, instead of being relieved by death, as some of them would be after his hearing. For these reasons, Eutychus languished in prison without a hearing.

Agrippa Bound

Some time later, Tiberius left Capreae and moved to Tusculanum, a city that was about twelve miles from Rome. Agrippa asked Antonia to get a hearing for Eutychus and end the matter one way or the other. Antonia was held in high regard by her brother-in-law Tiberius because she refused to remarry when her husband, Drusus the Great, died, even though she was still a young woman. Antonia had also informed Tiberius of a plot against him by Sejanus, one of her husband's friends who was a general of the army and had gained the support of many senate members and freedmen. Both of these actions had given her much influence with her brother-in-law.

When Antonia asked Tiberius to examine Eutychus, Tiberius delayed again, replying that Agrippa should be careful, especially if Eutychus was telling the truth. Despite this warning, Agrippa asked Antonia to continue pressuring Tiberius for the hearing. Finally Tiberius gave in and sent for Eutychus while Agrippa, Caius, and Antonia were in his presence, asking Eutychus what he had to say against Agrippa, the man who had given him his freedom. Eutychus replied that he had heard Agrippa tell Caius he couldn't wait until Tiberius and his grandson were out of the way and Caius were emperor, making the tale seem more sinister than it actually was.

Tiberius was already angry at Agrippa for ignoring his grandson Tiberius in favor of Caius; he told Macro (Sejanus's successor) to "bind this man" and left the room. Macro, not sure which man he had been ordered to bind and doubting it could be Agrippa, left him unbound until he received clearer instructions. Returning to find Agrippa still free, Tiberius repeated his instructions two more times, making it quite clear that Agrippa was the one to be bound and imprisoned.

The German's Prophecy

It was a very hot day, and Agrippa soon became thirsty. Seeing one of Caius's slaves, Thaumastus, carrying some water, Agrippa obtained a drink from him, promising to free him once he himself was free. Later Agrippa would keep this promise and free Thaumastus from Caius, making him the steward over his own estate and leaving him to his son Agrippa and daughter Bernice as their steward when he died. Thaumastus would grow old and die in that honorable position.

Agrippa stood before the palace with the other prisoners in bonds, leaning against a tree in grief. When an owl suddenly landed in the tree above him, a German prisoner asked a soldier who the prisoner dressed in royal purple was. Told his name was Agrippa and he was one of the most prominent men of Judea, the German asked permission of the guard to whom he was bound to speak to Agrippa. Given permission, the German spoke to Agrippa with the help of an interpreter, saying he knew Agrippa wouldn't believe him, but he had a prediction from the gods. Agrippa would soon be free of his bonds, the German said. He would be promoted to the highest position of dignity and power, and be envied by those who now pitied him, lead a happy life, and leave happiness to his children. But Agrippa should remember one thing: The next time he saw an owl, he would only have five days left to live. In return for this prophecy, the German only asked Agrippa to remember him in his happiness.

Agrippa laughed at the German's prophecy; he would later come to admire it.

Antonia was upset by her friend Agrippa's misfortune, but knew she could not change Tiberius's mind on the matter, so she talked to Macro, who was in charge of the soldiers guarding Agrippa. She convinced him to be kind to Agrippa, allow him to eat with the guards, bathe every day, and receive visitors. Agrippa's friend Silas and his two freedmen, Marsyas and Stechus, were allowed to bring him food and clothing during the six months he was imprisoned.

Tiberius's Decision

On his return to Capreae, Tiberius fell so sick that he despaired of recovering and ordered his favorite freedman, Euodus, to bring the two possible heirs to him before he died. Tiberius had no living sons; his only son, Drusus, had died. But his grandson, Tiberius Gemellus, was still living. Also still living was Caius (the son of Germanicus, Tiberius's nephew).

Caius was now a grown man, liberally educated and held in esteem by the people because of his father, Germanicus. Germanicus had always treated everyone as his equal, lived a virtuous life, and been widely loved throughout the Roman Empire; his death had been honestly mourned by everyone. The love the people felt toward Germanicus was to his son's advantage; so much so that the army was prepared to die for the sake of Caius, if that were needed to assure him the throne.

After Euodus left to summon the two men to Tiberius for the following morning, Tiberius prayed to his gods, asking them to give him a sign as to which man should be his heir. Personally, he wanted to leave the kingdom to his own grandson, but he also wanted to know the gods' wills on the matter, so he decided to leave the kingdom to the first of the two to arrive the next day. Hedging his bet, he then told his grandson's tutor to be sure Tiberius Gemellus arrived at the palace first thing in the morning.

Early the next day, Tiberius ordered Euodus to admit the first man that appeared. Euodus went out and found Caius in front of the door; Tiberius Gemellus had waited to eat his breakfast before appearing. On seeing Caius in front of him, Tiberius realized he was not fated to leave the kingdom to his grandson. Worse yet, he felt strongly that his grandson's life was in danger because of his decision.

Tiberius was deeply involved in astrology and impressed by predictions he had seen come true in his lifetime; now he was distressed by the destruction he foresaw for his grandson. He reproached himself for not using divination in his decision, positive that he would die an unhappy man because of the gods' decision. Nevertheless, he gave the kingdom to Caius, extracting a promise from him that no harm would come to Tiberius Gemellus. Caius gave his promise willingly, but once he was in control of the government, reneged on it and killed Tiberius Gemellus — the same fate that awaited him in the near future.

A few days after making Caius his heir, Tiberius died (March 16, 37). He had ruled for a total of twenty-two years, five months, and three days. Caius (who was better known as Caligula, his Roman nickname) became the fourth Roman emperor.

When the Romans heard rumors of Tiberius's death and Caligula's succession, they were afraid to show their joy, in case the news was not true, for Tiberius's temper was well-known and feared by all. The best families in Rome had suffered because of his fierce temper; his usual punishment for any offense, no matter how slight, was death.

As soon as he heard of Tiberius's death, Marsyas, Agrippa's freedman, ran to tell Agrippa the news, telling him in Hebrew, "The lion is dead." Agrippa, overjoyed at the news, thanked Marsyas for bringing it to him and said he hoped it was true. Agrippa's centurion guard saw their obvious happiness and asked what was going on. When they told him, he joined in their celebration and prepared a feast for them all, which ended suddenly when someone else appeared to claim Tiberius was still alive. The centurion could easily lose his life for his actions if Tiberius really were alive; he hastily rebound Agrippa. The following day, news of the death spread throughout the city, followed by letters from Caligula to the senate informing it of his succession. Agrippa was released from bonds and allowed to stay under house arrest in his own house until Caligula returned to Rome from Capreae.

Caligula arrived in Rome with Tiberius's body and arranged the royal funeral, planning to release Agrippa immediately until Antonia showed him that would seem disrespectful of Tiberius. A few days later, Caligula sent for his friend Agrippa, put a diadem on his head, and appointed him king of Philip's tetrarchy. He promised him the tetrarchy of Lysanias and changed his iron chain for a golden one of equal weight. At the same time, Caligula appointed Marullus the procurator of Judea.

In the second year of Caligula's reign, Agrippa asked and received permission to return to his kingdom and set his affairs there in order. He returned unexpectedly as a king, which made many who remembered him as a pauper wonder at his great change of fortune.

Herodias's Jealousy

Seeing that her brother Agrippa now possessed more authority in Judea than her husband, Herod the tetrarch, Herodias soon became jealous and ambitious. It particularly bothered her to see Agrippa out amid the crowds with all his flags and other outward signs of royalty. She encouraged Herod to sail to Rome and seek a position equal to Agrippa's, telling him she couldn't bear to live as an inferior to her brother. After all, she complained, Agrippa was Aristobulus's son, and Herod the

74

Great had had Aristobulus killed; her husband was Herod's own son. Besides, when Agrippa had come to them in extreme poverty, hadn't they had to support him? Agrippa had fled from his creditors to return a king; certainly Herod deserved as much, if not more! They must invest their riches in obtaining a kingdom for themselves.

Herod denied Herodias's requests at this point, partly out of laziness and partly because he thought going to Rome would cause more problems than it would solve. The more he shrank from going, the more Herodias nagged him, until she made it quite clear she would continue nagging until he gave in. Herod gave in, traveling to Rome in royal style.

As soon as Agrippa heard Herod had sailed, he sent Fortunatus, one of his freedmen, after him, carrying presents and letters for Caligula and instructing Fortunatus to tell Caligula of Herod's ambitions if he should have the opportunity. Fortunatus left so soon after Herod and had such a fast trip that he delivered his gifts and letters to Caligula while Herod was with him.

Both had sailed to Dicearchia and caught up with Caligula in Baiae, a little city of Campania about half a mile from Dicearchia. Baiae not only had royal palaces with luxurious apartments, but also boasted hot springs beneficial to the health of those who bathed in them.

The letters sent by Agrippa accused Herod of having taken part in Sejanus's plot against Tiberius and of now plotting with Artabanus, the king of Parthia, against Caligula. As proof of Herod's complicity, Agrippa told Caligula that Herod possessed enough armor to outfit 70,000 men.

When Caligula asked Herod if he really did have that much armor at hand, Herod was forced to admit he did, since it was common knowledge. Caligula took this as proof that Herod was planning to revolt. He took away Herod's tetrarchy and gave it to Agrippa, gave all his money to Agrippa, and banished Herod to Lyons (France) for the remainder of his life.

Hearing that Herodias was Agrippa's sister, Caligula said she could keep whatever money was her own and escape banishment, but Herodias politely refused, saying her love for

Herod would not allow her to take Caligula's gift. She had been Herod's partner in his prosperity, she said; now she would be his partner in his misfortune. In reply, Caligula sent her into banishment with Herod and gave her estate to Agrippa.

Thus did God punish Herodias for her envy of her brother and Herod for listening to her advice.

During the first and second years of his reign, Caligula managed public affairs with such justice and moderation that he gained the goodwill of the Romans and his other subjects, but as time went on, his pride and conceit corrupted him until he believed himself to be a god.

Petronius

Trouble had arisen in Alexandria between the Jews and the Greeks living there, so three men from each side went to plead their cases before Caligula. Speaking for the Greeks, Apion uttered many blasphemies against the Jews, including the accusation that they refused to give Caesar the honor due him. Apion reminded Caligula that all Roman subjects built altars and temples to him and treated him as a god; only the Jews refused to erect statues to him or swear by his name.

Philo, the principal Jewish ambassador, was ready to speak and quite capable of defending his people against these accusations, but Caligula was so angry that he sent him away. Philo told the Jews outside not to worry: Caligula was angry at them, but he had already set God against himself.

Caligula was furious at the Jews. How dare they refuse to show him the respect he deserved? He appointed Petronius to succeed Vitellius as president of Syria, ordering him to take his troops into Judea and erect his statue in the temple. If the Jews accepted it peacefully, fine; if not, Petronius should go to war and force them to accept Caligula's statue.

Petronius promptly took over the government of Syria, raised as many auxiliary soldiers as he could, and took them with two Roman legions to Ptolemais, where he intended to spend the winter before beginning the war in the spring. He reported his actions to Caligula, who commended him for acting so promptly and reaffirmed his order to erect the statue.

Protests in Ptolemais and Tiberius

Thousands of Jews came to Ptolemais to petition Petronius not to force them to disobey the law of their forefathers. If he must erect the statue in their temple, they asked him to at least kill them first.

Petronius replied that the Jews had no right to petition him. He was not Caesar, he was a soldier under orders he could not disobey without losing his life. The Jews said they were in exactly the same position; they could not disobey their laws without losing their lives. But if they showed God they were willing to suffer to uphold His laws, He would help them.

Seeing the determination of the Jews and realizing he would have to use force to erect Caligula's statue, Petronius traveled to Tiberius to see if the Jews there were equally adamant. Thousands of them made the same petition in Tiberius that was made in Ptolemais. Petronius asked them if they were determined to make war with Caesar over the issue, even though they would obviously lose, to which they replied they had no intention of making war; all they intended to do was die before their laws were transgressed. For the next forty days, the Jews of Tiberius threw themselves to the ground before Petronius, baring their necks and saying they were ready to die. In the meantime, their fields were not being worked, even though it was time for them to be seeded.

Petronius's Decision

While the stalemate continued, Aristobulus (King Agrippa's brother), Helcias the Great, and other leaders of that family went to Petronius and asked him not to do anything before writing to Caesar. Caesar should be told how determined the Jews were and how the whole country would suffer if the land were not seeded — also how Caligula would not be able to collect his tribute if the crops failed.

Petronius did not want to kill thousands of unresisting Jews merely to satisfy Caligula's vanity, but he knew writing to Caligula in hopes of changing his mind was extremely dangerous. Caligula's orders were to be obeyed, not argued with. But if risking his life by sending the letter would save thousands of lives, it was a risk worth taking.

Petronius called the Jews together in Tiberius and arranged his army in front of them. He told the crowd about Caesar's orders and how Caesar would react to any disobedience on his part or theirs. Then he said he did not feel it just to preserve his own life if it meant the death of so many of them. With God's help, Petronius would try to prevent the temple from being defaced. He promised to write to Caligula in hopes of changing his orders, but if Caligula turned his anger on him for disobeying, he would willingly take his punishment before killing them. He urged the Jews to go back to their land while he did what he could to help them.

This whole year had been one of drought. The day Petronius made this speech was another clear, cloudless, dry day. But as soon as Petronius finished speaking, God sent down great showers of rain, which the Jews saw as a sign that Petronius would be successful in saving them. Even Petronius and the other Romans present were impressed by God's care of the faithful Jews.

Petronius wrote his letter to Caligula, telling him of the Jews' resolve to die before seeing God's laws broken. This would certainly cause a great loss of revenue for Caligula, he reminded him. Moreover, the Jews' God had shown His support of the Jews in this matter, which was why Petronius was writing to ask Caligula to change his orders.

Agrippa's Feast

At this time, King Agrippa was living in Rome in great favor with Caligula. One evening Agrippa held a great feast for his friend, one so lavish and expensive that it was obviously beyond his means. Even Caligula would have had trouble paying for a meal that expensive, and he knew it. Feeling Agrippa should be rewarded for his extreme generosity, and also being drunk at the time, Caligula apologized for not being generous enough to his friend and told him to ask for anything he wanted. A large country, new revenues — anything he asked, Caligula would grant.

Agrippa knew exactly what he wanted. First he assured Caligula his friendship had always been genuine, even when Tiberius had opposed it. He wanted nothing for himself. Caligula had already been more than generous to him.

Surprised by Agrippa's lack of greed, Caligula insisted he request something of him. Agrippa continued to say he wanted nothing for himself, but he would make a request that, if granted, would enlarge Caligula's reputation for piety and assure him of the help of the gods in any future ventures. He asked him to rescind Petronius's orders to erect his statue in the temple at Jerusalem. Agrippa knew very well that he was placing his life in danger with this request, but believed the matter was worth the risk.

Caligula was pleased with Agrippa's loyalty to him and his virtue in not requesting anything for personal gain. Agrippa was an excellent king, an old friend he could trust. Besides, Caligula would lose face if he refused this humble request when he had openly offered Agrippa anything he wanted in front of witnesses.

Caligula wrote to Petronius. If the statue was already up, leave it, he said. If not, dismiss the army and forget the whole thing.

Caligula wrote this letter to Petronius before receiving Petronius's letter to him about the rebelliousness of the Jews. On later receiving that letter, Caligula, displeased that anyone would disobey his orders and at heart a vicious man who enjoyed venting his anger, told Petronius that if he preferred to listen to the Jews than obey his emperor, he should be his own judge, for he intended to make an example of him to others who might dare to question his orders.

This letter, which in effect ordered Petronius to commit suicide, was delayed and did not reach Petronius until other letters arrived saying Caligula was dead. God did not forget

Petronius's honor and the danger he had put himself in for the law of the Jews. Petronius rejoiced at the good timing of Caligula's death and admired God's providence in rewarding his efforts.

Asineus and Anileus

There was a city in Babylonia named Neerda, which was not only large and filled with men of fighting age, but well protected from assault by its walls and the Euphrates River, which totally encircled it. Another city nearby, similarly protected, was named Nisibis. Because of the natural protection enjoyed by these two cities, the Jews in the area used them as storehouses for their temple offerings — the half shekel that every Jew donated and other valuable articles. At the proper time, these collected treasures would be taken to Jerusalem under guard to avoiding having them stolen by the Parthians who ruled Babylonia at the time.

Two brothers named Asineus and Anileus were living in Neerda. Their father being dead, their mother arranged to have them learn the art of weaving curtains, which was an acceptable occupation for men in that area. Arriving late for work one day, the brothers were whipped by their master. Angry and insulted by this punishment, the two brothers stole the many weapons kept in their master's house and fled to a spot where the river divided — a place naturally suited for keeping the city's cattle and preserving fruits for the winter. They were joined there by other poor young men, whom they armed and led in raids throughout the area. As soon as they were strong enough and had built themselves a fortification, they sent to those who kept their cattle in the area, demanding tribute from them. The brothers promised to protect the cattle owners who provided for their needs; those who refused would find their cattle killed. Because they could do nothing else, the owners sent them as many sheep as they requested.

The band grew stronger and stronger as it continued its attacks on the area, taking whatever land they desired until no one dared oppose them.

80

The governor of Babylonia decided these men had to be stopped before they became even more powerful and dangerous; he quietly raised an army of Parthians and Babylonians and marched against the brothers, hoping to surprise them. Arriving in the area on the day before the Sabbath, the governor waited until the next day before moving his army closer. He knew the Jewish prohibition against fighting on the Sabbath and expected to take the brothers without a fight, especially if he could surprise them.

Asineus was the first in the camp to hear the approaching army's horses and bridles. He sent scouts out, hoping he was wrong; the returning scouts confirmed Asineus's suspicions and declared that they were defeated, since they could not fight the approaching army on the Sabbath.

Asineus didn't agree with his scouts' evaluation of the situation. The way he saw it, the law would be better served if they died fighting instead of submitting to their own massacre. Rallying his men around him, he defeated the Babylonian governor's army, Sabbath or no Sabbath.

Artabanus

Hearing of the battle, the king of Parthia was impressed by the brothers' boldness. He sent his guards to urge Asineus and Anileus to come see him, guaranteeing their safety on the trip. Asineus refused to go, but he allowed Anileus to make the trip and provided him with as many presents for the king as he could find. When Artabanus saw Anileus arriving alone, he sent him back for his brother, taking an oath on his gods that no harm would come to them and giving him his right hand, a sure sign among the Parthians that their word could be trusted.

Artabanus was eager to make peace with the brothers because his own provinces were threatening to revolt. He couldn't afford to have the brothers making any alliances with his rebellious governors or taking advantage of his absence if he should have to put down a revolt in another area.

Anileus convinced Asineus it was safe to go to Artabanus, who made them both welcome. Artabanus was particularly impressed by Anileus's courage, since Anileus was a small man, not at all imposing, and very common looking. *Anileus's body may be inferior, but he certainly possesses a superior soul,* the king thought.

Abdagases, one of Artabanus's generals, was not all that impressed, however, and asked permission to kill Asineus. Artabanus would not allow his word to be broken, but if Abdagases wanted to attack the brothers once they had safely returned home, that was his business — as long as Artabanus didn't know anything about it in advance.

Artabanus put all of Babylonia under the protection of the two brothers before sending them home. As soon as he returned home, Asineus built himself more fortifications and rose to great power in the area faster than anyone before him had ever done. He was treated with respect by both the Parthians and the Babylonians, governing the whole area of Mesopotamia for the next fifteen years.

The Foreign Wife

Although their public affairs were flourishing, the brothers were neglecting the laws that had made them great and falling under the power of lust and pleasure. Anileus fell in love with the beautiful and talented wife of a Parthian general in the area. When her husband died in a battle against the brothers, she was carried off as a captive, bringing with her the family's idols. At first she worshiped her idols in private, but after Anileus married her, she worshiped them openly.

Anileus's friends warned him of the danger of allowing his foreign wife to openly worship her idols, saying that he had come to power because of God's blessing; now his whole life was a mockery of God. Angry at being reproved, Anileus had one of his best friends killed for his boldness, but not before the man cursed both brothers and their followers for transgressing the law.

A number of men went to Asineus when they heard about Anileus's wife and asked him to correct Anileus's ways before they all suffered the consequences. Asineus was well aware of

82

his brother's transgression of the law and the problems it was causing in the army, yet he had chosen to overlook it out of love for his brother. Eventually, as the complaints continued to come, he told Anileus that he had to send his wife back to her people, an order that was never carried out because Anileus's wife panicked and poisoned Asineus.

Now totally in charge of the government, Anileus led his army against villages belonging to Mithridates, Artabanus's son-in-law, a man high in the Parthian government. Mithridates had done Anileus no harm and was rightfully offended at having his villages plundered. He gathered together an army to fight Anileus and held it in one of his villages, planning to attack on the Sabbath. Warned of Mithridates's plan, Anileus attacked the village in the middle of the night, captured Mithridates alive, and set him naked on an ass, which is the greatest insult possible to a Parthian.

Although Mithridates was humiliated, Anileus would not allow his followers to kill him. Mithridates was a member of a royal family, he said, and Artabanus would certainly seek revenge if they killed him, probably killing many Babylonian Jews in the process. Anileus reminded his followers that they needed the goodwill of their fellow Jews in case it was ever necessary for them to seek safety among them. Mithridates was released and sent to his home.

Mithridates was quite happy to have escaped with his life and not at all anxious for revenge, but his wife was outraged. How could he, the son-in-law of a king, not avenge himself on those who had humiliated him? He would either go back and fight like a man or she would divorce him. Unwillingly, Mithridates reassembled his army and marched on Anileus. He didn't want to fight, but neither did he want to be in a position of owing his life to the Jews.

Hearing that Mithridates was on his way, Anileus set out to meet him. In addition to his army, he was joined by many others, some who hoped to grow rich through plundering, others who wanted to be part of a great victory. Their path lay over very dry, sandy territory, and in the middle of the day, when they were extremely thirsty and tired, Mithridates attacked and routed Anileus's army, slaughtering many of them.

Anileus and some of his followers escaped into a wood, where they were soon joined by a large number of desperate men looking for a leader who could bring them some prosperity. These new men were so many in number that they made up for those he had lost in the battle, but they were undisciplined and inexperienced fighters.

Anileus and his new army attacked the Babylonian villages so severely that the Babylonians sent ambassadors to the Jews in Neerda, demanding they surrender Anileus. The Jews of Neerda weren't in a position to surrender Anileus, even if they wanted to, but they thought it would be a good idea to at least try to make peace with the Babylonians, so they took the ambassadors to talk with Anileus. Now the Babylonians knew exactly where Anileus was. Late one night, while his soldiers were drunk and asleep, the Babylonians attacked, killing everyone they caught, including Anileus.

The Babylonians and the Jews had long hated each other because their laws were so different, but Anileus's strength had protected the Jews for years. Now that he was gone, the Babylonians renewed their attacks on the Jews, driving them to Seleucia for refuge. Seleucia was populated mainly by Greeks, although Macedonians and Syrians also lived there. The Jews lived there in peace for the next five years.

The Greeks and the Syrians living in Seleucia did not get along with each other, but the Greeks outnumbered the Syrians. The newly arrived Jews could easily change the balance of power if they joined the Syrians, so the Greeks set about to prevent that from happening. They sent ambassadors to the Syrians and arranged a peace with them, which left the Jews with no allies in the city and two strong enemies. Both the Greeks and the Syrians attacked the Jews, killing about 50,000 of them; the few remaining Jews in Babylonia escaped to safety in Neerda and Nisibis.

SIX

Caligula's madness not only brought trouble to the Jews in Jerusalem, but affected the whole Roman Empire, especially the city of Rome itself. Rome's most prominent citizens — its senators, nobility, and members of the civil service — were often singled out for execution and their estates confiscated by the emperor.

By now, Caligula was claiming to be a god, the brother of Jupiter, in fact, and insisting his subjects treat him as a god. Other actions also indicated he had gone beyond the bounds of reason. He built a bridge nearly four miles long over the bay connecting the cities of Dicearchia and Misenum so he would not have to travel between the cities in a rowboat. He was emperor of the sea as well as the land; the sea would bow to his will. He plundered Greek temples and had their statues and wealth sent to him in Rome, as well as anything he fancied in the houses that sheltered him during his travels.

He ordered Memmius Regulus to move the statue of Jupiter Olympius, which had been carved by Phidias the Athenian, to Rome, but Regulus delayed on the advice of architects who said the statue couldn't be moved, and Caligula was dead before the move was attempted.

When Caligula's wife had a baby daughter, he took her to the temple of Jupiter, placed her upon the knees of Jupiter's statue, and declared himself and Jupiter her joint fathers.

Caligula also gave Roman slaves permission to accuse their masters of any crimes they chose, which they gladly did, since they saw it pleased the emperor. Even Caligula's own uncle Claudius was accused by his slave Pollux; Caligula attended his trial, hoping to see his uncle condemned to death, but that was not the outcome. The whole Roman Empire was thrown into a turmoil of false accusations and terror until the slaves were actually ruling their masters with Caligula's permission.

The Conspirators

Three main conspiracies soon began to take shape against Caligula, all led by highly eminent men. The first leader was Emilius Regulus, a bold man from Corduba, Spain, who was dedicated to freedom. Minucianus Annius, whose friend Lepidus had been killed by Caligula, was the second leader. The third was Cherea Cassius, the tribune of the pretorian guard. Of the three, Cherea was the most zealous and, as the closest to Caligula, the one with the most opportunity. All three men had collected their own groups of co-conspirators, men who had not only suffered under Caligula but were willing to die to free the empire from his madness.

It was the time of the horse races (the Circensian games), when emperors had traditionally granted the Roman crowds their petitions. The crowd at the games this year begged Caligula to relieve them of some of their taxes. When he refused, they continued to petition him until he ordered his troops to pull out the troublemakers and execute them, which they did, killing a great number. Seeing the slaughter made Cherea more determined than ever to kill Caligula, and although he could easily have killed him as he feasted, he waited for a surer opportunity.

Cherea's Humiliation

Cherea had been in the army a long time, but he wasn't happy to find himself in a trusted position so close to the emperor, who had sent him out to collect overdue taxes for his treasury. Since the taxes had recently been doubled, Cherea delayed in collecting them from people he knew could not afford to pay and was generally less aggressive than he should have been, in Caligula's eyes. Caligula reprimanded him for his laziness and lack of masculinity in tax collecting.

As commander of the guard, it was part of Cherea's job to receive the password from Caligula, who took these occasions to humiliate Cherea by giving him effeminate passwords. Cherea had no choice but to communicate the passwords to his troops, which soon made him the butt of their coarse jokes. Caligula took great delight in seeing the commander of his guards totally embarrassed, although Caligula himself quite often wore women's clothing and did other things that made him seem effeminate. All this only made Cherea more determined to kill Caligula.

Pompedius, a Roman senator, had charges brought against him by his enemy Timidius, who accused him before Caligula of using "indecent reproaches" against him. As a witness, Timidius called Quintilia, a popular and beautiful actress who was in love with Pompedius; Quintilia refused to lie about her lover. Timidius, implying that Caligula had not done all he could to secure the witness's cooperation, asked that she be tortured.

Knowing that Cherea would do almost anything to disprove the rumors going around about his lack of masculinity, Caligula routinely gave him the responsibility of torturing witnesses; he could be counted on to be brutal. Left with no choice, Cherea tortured Quintilia unmercifully before bringing her back to Caligula. The once-beautiful woman was so physically destroyed that even Caligula was moved by the sight of her. He freed her and Pompedius and gave her money as payment for her suffering.

Cherea was more than upset by having to torture people so severely that even Caligula had pity on them. He spoke of his shame to Clement, a general of the army, and Papinius, a tribune. Although Clement held his tongue, it was obvious to Cherea that he, too, was ashamed of supporting the emperor in his tyranny. Cherea continued, saying they could all blame Caligula, but the fault was really theirs. Not only were they obeying Caligula's brutal orders, they were actually giving their consent to his actions when they didn't take advantage of their opportunities to kill him and free the empire. The weapons they bore were not for the sake of liberty or preserving the government, but only for preserving the life of a man who had enslaved their bodies and their minds and who polluted them with the blood of others every day. Eventually, Cherea warned, they too would fall by Caligula's hand, unless they procured the liberty and safety of all Roman citizens.

Clement openly approved of Cherea's intentions but urged him to watch his tongue, or the plot would be exposed before it could be successful. As for himself, he would help where he could, but he was too old to make an attempt on Caligula's life.

Cherea spoke next to Cornelius Sabinus, another tribune whom he knew was upset by the state of affairs. Sabinus had been making his own plans but hadn't dared mention them to anyone; the two of them went together to Minucianus, one of Rome's most outstanding and respected citizens. Minucianus sent them off with his support and good wishes, which were exactly what Cherea needed. Leaving the house, Cherea heard a voice from the crowd encouraging him to take the opportunity providence had provided and finish what he had started. He wasn't sure if the voice was that of a betrayer, a supporter, or a god; either way, it helped his determination.

The plot was revealed to more and more people: senators, soldiers, civil servants. Even Callistus, one of Caligula's own freedmen who had grown rich and powerful in his service, heard of it. He immediately transferred his allegiance to Claudius in expectation of his assuming the throne on Caligula's death.

Delays

As eager as Cherea was to have Caligula dead before they were all discovered, action was delayed day after day, despite many opportunities. It could have been done while Caligula was in the temple of Jupiter making sacrifices for his daughter.

He could have been pushed off the top of the palace on those occasions when he threw gold and silver pieces down to the crowd. Even without his sword, Cherea knew he had many opportunities to kill Caligula.

His co-conspirators knew Cherea was right, but they urged him to wait until the shows were given at the palace in celebration of Augustus Caesar. Great crowds would be gathered to see the shows, and Caligula would attend; the crowded conditions would prevent the guards from protecting the emperor properly. Cherea agreed to the delay, but when the shows began, they could find no opportunity to attack.

Early on the final day of the shows (January 24, 41), Cherea called his co-conspirators together, shaming them for putting off what they all knew had to be done and reminding them that Caligula would soon leave for Egypt. How would they all feel if some Egyptian did their work for them? With or without their help, Cherea would kill Caligula that day. Seeing his determination, everyone agreed to do his part.

The Shows

Cherea reported to the palace wearing his sword, which he was expected to do on the days he received a new password. The crowds were already there, jostling for position outside and for seats inside the theater. Caligula came out of the palace to offer a sacrifice to Augustus Caesar, and during the ceremony, a priest helping with the sacrifice slipped and splattered blood all over the clothes of Asprenas, one of the senators who was in the conspiracy with Cherea. Caligula thought it great fun to see a noble Roman senator covered in blood, but then everyone present noticed that the emperor was in an extraordinarily good mood that day as he went in to see the show with his friends.

Caligula enjoyed the day's shows, since they were extremely violent stories with an abundance of false blood spread all over the stage. He also enjoyed seeing the crowds scramble for the autumn fruit and rare birds that were tossed into the audience. But it was the last day of the shows, and he was thinking about leaving for a bath and dinner, then returning for the end of the show.

Minucianus, who was sitting behind Caligula, saw that Cherea had left the theater and got up to join him, but Caligula took hold of him and told him to stay. A little while later, Minucianus tried again; this time Caligula let him go. Asprenas, still covered with the sacrificial blood and anxious to get it over with, urged Caligula to leave for his bath and dinner.

Meanwhile, Cherea and his men outside were becoming impatient and worried that their absence would be noticed. Cherea decided he would kill Caligula in his seat, if necessary, even though it would mean a great loss of life. Just as they started back in, word came that Caligula was leaving; Cherea and his men pushed the crowd back out of the way. Caligula's uncle, Claudius, came out first, followed by Marcus Vinicius and Valerius of Asia. The conspirators thought it would be safer to eliminate them all, but their respect for these people kept them from acting.

Finally, Caligula and Paulus Arruntius came out. Caligula turned into a private narrow passageway to the baths, where Cherea met him and asked for the new password.

Caligula gave Cherea one of his ridiculous passwords, at which point Cherea rebuked him, drew his sword, and struck Caligula a blow to the chest. This blow did not kill Caligula, since it hit the breastbone, but it doubled him over in pain as he tried to escape without either crying out in pain or calling for help.

Cornelius Sabinus pushed Caligula to his knees and the conspirators attacked him with their swords; the fatal blow came from Aquila.

The Aftermath

Cherea and his men broke up and fled through the narrow passageways before the crowd or soldiers noticed that Caligula was dead, hiding in the house originally built for Germanicus, Caligula's father.

The first to discover that Caligula was dead were his personal guards, the Germans. The men of that country are naturally passionate and strong, fierce in battle, and these guards were loyal to Caligula, who had paid them well for their affection. One of the tribunes named Sabinus led the Germans in their search for the murderers. The first man they found and killed was Asprenas, still covered with the blood from the sacrifice. The second was Norbanus, a strong man who fought bravely before his death. The third to die was Anteius, a senator who hated Caligula so much that he came out to see his body and was then unable to escape the thorough search the Germans were making of all the houses.

Those people still in the theater were astonished to hear rumors of Caligula's death, and although many were happy at the news, no one dared show his feelings in case the rumor proved false. Some in the theater were upset by the news. The soldiers who had gained honors by carrying out his orders were not anxious to see Caligula dead, nor were the women and children who he entertained with shows and presents or the slaves who looked forward to accusing their masters and receiving one-eighth of their estates as a reward. Rumors spread through the theater. One said Caligula was alive and being cared for by physicians; another that he was wounded but speaking to the crowd in the marketplace.

Still the crowd kept their seats, afraid to go out and be accused of joining the plot. Soon the Germans surrounded the theater with their swords drawn, until the whole crowd inside feared for their lives whether they stayed or left. When the Germans entered the theater, the crowd begged for mercy, saying they had done nothing wrong. Why weren't the soldiers out looking for the murderers instead of threatening them? Calmed slightly by the pleas of the crowd, the Germans put the heads of Asprenas and those killed with him on the altar and stood their ground, although they refrained from harming the terrified crowd.

The public crier in the market at this time was a man named Euaristus Arruntius. He was a very wealthy man, able to do whatever he pleased in the city. Although he hated Caligula as much as anyone else, he dressed himself in the most mournful clothing he could find, concealed his pleasure, and came to the theater to publicly announce the death. When he had made his announcement, he called the Germans to put up their swords, and thus he saved the crowd. The Germans would gladly have died for Caligula, but once he was dead, he could no longer reward them or protect them from the discipline of the senate.

Before the Germans had been pacified, Cherea worried about the safety of Minucianus so much that he went to all the soldiers and inquired about him, asking them to protect Minucianus from the Germans, should they find him. When Minucianus was found and brought safely to General Clement, he and the senators present let him go, saying the conspirators had done the right thing. Although they may have done the actual killing, they said, Caligula had brought on his own death by his actions. The senate had also met and begun its search for the killers, but they searched in name only, having no desire to punish anyone.

Once the people in the theater realized they were out of danger, they panicked in their rush to leave, then started their own search for Caligula's killers. Meeting Valerius of Asia, they asked him who had done the killing, to which he replied, "I wish I had been the man."

Soon the consuls published an edict accusing Caligula and urging everyone, including the soldiers, to return to their homes and cause no more problems in the city.

Cesonia's Death

While public affairs were in this unsettled condition, the soldiers gathered for a meeting to debate what should be done. They believed a democratic government would have difficulty managing the complex empire and would not be in their own best interest; they decided they should not delay in declaring Claudius the new emperor. Claudius was Caligula's uncle, a man well-loved by the senators because of his illustrious family and his own excellent education. The soldiers were anxious to show their loyalty to the most probable candidate for emperor in hopes of being generously rewarded, so they hurried Claudius away from his house and kept him under protection.

Meanwhile the senate was meeting. Cneus Sentius Saturninus knew that Claudius was planning to accept the soldiers' proclamation, even though he was pretending unwillingness. Saturninus addressed the senate, rejoicing in the sudden return of liberty and the end of the tyrannical rule they had endured since Caesar's time. He himself had never lived under liberty, he said, but he welcomed it as an opportunity for virtuous and happy living, even if it might be short-lived. Then he reminded his fellow senators of the injustices they had known under every emperor. Now was the time for the senate to speak and act freely, instead of keeping silent in fear of a tyrant.

In the first place, he said, the senate should reward Caligula's assassins, especially Cherea Cassius, who had risked his life to secure them their present freedom. Further, the senate should declare that Cherea had acted from the beginning with their approval. It was only right to reward the man who freed Rome from tyranny.

The senators and those civil servants who were present received Sentius's speech warmly. Trebellius Maximus, seeing that Sentius still wore a ring he had forgotten that bore Caligula's image, took the ring off his finger and smashed it.

By now it was late at night; Cherea asked the consuls for his watchword. They told him the word was *liberty,* realizing this was the first time in one hundred years that the consuls had been asked to perform this particular duty, which was theirs by law. Ever since Caesar, the soldiers had been commanded by the emperor, not by the civil authorities. Cherea delivered the password to the four regiments remaining loyal to the senate and opposed to the succession of an emperor; the soldiers and the crowd retired, rejoicing in their restored freedom.

But Cherea was uneasy about the fact that Caligula's wife and daughter were still alive, fearing they might cause trouble, so he proposed to send Julius Lupus, a tribune, to kill them. Lupus was chosen because he was related to Clement and the conspirators wanted Clement to share in their glory.

Not all the conspirators agreed that Caligula's wife should be killed. Some said she approved of and encouraged Caligula's brutality, but others said he was just naturally brutal. In the end, Cherea prevailed and Lupus was sent to kill her.

Arriving at the palace, Lupus found Cesonia lying on the ground beside Caligula's body, smeared with his blood and bewailing her fate. Her daughter lay beside her. Cesonia was telling the dead Caligula that he should have listened to what she had told him. Even the people present disagreed about the meaning of her words. Was she saying she'd warned Caligula about his barbarity and cruelty? Or had she heard of the plot and warned him, only to have her warnings ignored?

When she saw Lupus approaching, Cesonia showed him Caligula's body and motioned him closer while she cried. Then she realized Lupus was there on an errand he found distasteful. She bared her throat to him and told him not to hesitate in sealing her appointed fate; Lupus killed both her and her daughter, as ordered.

Caligula had reigned for three years and eight months (A.D. 37-41). Even before he was emperor, he was ill-natured and wicked, a slave to his pleasures, a lover of lies, a man of murderous disposition. His wealth came from murder and injustice; he enjoyed using his exorbitant power to insolently injure those who least deserved it. Although he tried to appear above consideration of human or divine laws, he was a slave to the flattery of his subjects.

Whatever the laws declared to be shameful or punished, he esteemed virtuous. No matter how friendly he appeared toward a person or how good that person's character, Caligula would punish at the slightest provocation. Any man who endeavored to lead a virtuous life was Caligula's enemy. Nothing he commanded could be contradicted. He even had sexual relations with his own sister, which caused the citizens to hate him because that sort of incest had not been known for some time.

As for any great works that might benefit the present or future, only one could be found: the haven for ships bringing wheat from Egypt that he began around Rhegium and Sicily. While this work was useful and good in itself, it was only half completed; Caligula preferred to spend his money on his own pleasures.

Caligula was an excellent orator, thoroughly acquainted with both the Greek and Roman languages. He was persuasive when he chose to be because of his studied and practiced affability. Since Tiberius valued and encouraged education, Caligula took his studies seriously and aspired to eloquence. But all the advantages of his education could not overcome the problems he brought on himself by exercising his authority; it is difficult for a man with absolute power to live virtuously and wisely.

At first, while he dedicated himself to learning and worthy actions, he was surrounded and loved by worthy friends, but when he became insolent to them, they came to hate him, and from that hatred sprang the plot that destroyed him.

Claudius and the Soldiers

At the time of Caligula's murder, Claudius had left the theater just ahead of the emperor. During the disturbance that followed, he hid himself. Not that he had any reason to suspect he was a target — he was a private citizen living modestly and occupied with studying the Greeks — but because of the general disorder. The crowd, the soldiers, even the emperor's guards were all filled with fear and consternation. The pretorian guards were trying to decide what they should do next. They were not particularly upset by Caligula's well-deserved death, but they had to look out for their own welfare. The Germans were busy slaughtering Caligula's murderers, a job they seemed to be enjoying very much.

Claudius was afraid for his safety, especially when he saw the Germans carrying around the heads of Asprenas and his friends. He hid in the shadows a few steps above where Caligula had been attacked.

Gratus, one of the palace soldiers, saw Claudius hiding in the shadows. He moved closer until he recognized him, then called out to his followers, "This is a Germanicus. Come on, let's choose him as our emperor."

Seeing the soldiers were preparing to take him away by force, Claudius begged them to spare him, reminding them that he led a quiet life and had nothing to do with Caligula or his death. Gratus took Claudius's right hand, smiled at him, and told him to stop worrying about saving himself. He should be thinking greater things, even of obtaining the empire that the gods were committing to his care. "Go to, therefore, and accept of the throne of thy ancestors," he urged. Because Claudius was too upset to walk, the soldiers picked him up and carried him.

A large number of guards had gathered around Gratus, some of whom thought Claudius was being taken to his death. They knew him to be a private citizen uninvolved in politics and decided the consuls should know his life was in danger. When they asked the men carrying Claudius why he was being taken away, those carrying him fled, and the soldiers carried Claudius into the palace court. More and more soldiers gathered around, all of whom thought it fitting that Claudius should be the next emperor, since he was the brother of Germanicus, a man everyone had loved and respected.

The soldiers were also concerned about leaving the government in the hands of the senate, knowing many senators to be greedy men capable of misrule. There was a very real danger that someone might be made emperor without their help, which would leave them vulnerable to punishment and unrewarded, while Claudius was sure to be generous. The general consensus among the soldiers seemed to be that Claudius should be proclaimed emperor and then protected. Claudius was hastily carried into camp surrounded by soldiers who took turns carrying his chair.

The senate disagreed with the soldiers' solution; they wanted to keep their newfound freedom and authority. The populace seemed to support Claudius, who they hoped could prevent a civil war from erupting among the ambitious senators who would otherwise vie for power among themselves.

The senators sent two ambassadors to Claudius: Veranius and Brocchus, both tribunes of the people. They asked Claudius not to take the throne by force, but to let the law rule the city. If he would live quietly, the senate would confer the greatest of honors on him; if not, they would prevent him from becoming emperor by force. They reminded Claudius that they had a large part of the army and numerous weapons and slaves at their disposal. Falling to their knees, Veranius and Brocchus begged Claudius not to throw the city into civil war.

However, the two men soon saw that the crowd of soldiers guarding Claudius was more numerous than those supporting the senate. They modified their demands: If Claudius did desire to rule, it would be better if he accepted power from the senate, rather than taking it by force. Even though Claudius felt insulted by the senate's insolence, he did nothing rash for the moment.

Agrippa

Agrippa had paid Caligula the respect due an honored friend. He went to the palace, embraced the body, laid it on a bed and covered it as well as he could, then went out and told the guard Caligula was still alive but in need of a physician.

Hearing that Claudius had been carried off by the soldiers, Agrippa rushed through the crowd to the camp. At this point, Claudius was still upset and ready to give the government to the senate, but Agrippa encouraged him not to let the office slip out of his hands when it seemed to be coming to him so easily. After speaking to Claudius so encouragingly, Agrippa returned to his home.

Shortly thereafter, the senate sent for him. He anointed his head with ointment so it would appear he had been making love to his wife (instead of talking to Claudius) and went to them, asking where Claudius was at the moment. The senate told Agrippa how things stood and asked for his opinion regarding the government.

Agrippa assured the senators he would willingly give his life for the honor and freedom of the senate, but asked if they had thought the matter through completely. If they intended to take control of the government, they needed weapons and soldiers to guard them. When the senate replied that they could obtain weapons and money and augment their loyal forces by freeing the needed number of slaves, Agrippa explained that an untrained army of slaves was no match for Claudius's seasoned troops. It would be better to send ambassadors to Claudius and ask him to lay down the government. As for himself, he was ready to serve as one of the senate's ambassadors.

The senate agreed to Agrippa's suggestion and made him one of their ambassadors to Claudius, but in the meantime, Agrippa secretly informed Claudius of the disorder the senate was in, advising him to speak to the ambassadors with dignity and authority.

Claudius told the ambassadors he understood why they did not want another emperor over them; they had been treated barbarically by former rulers. But he would provide a fair government and peaceful times, ruling only in name and sharing authority with the senators. They should trust him; they had known him all his life. Then he dismissed the ambassadors.

The soldiers with Claudius all took an oath of loyalty to him after he addressed them. As a reward, Claudius gave every man present five thousand drachmae — more to the captains — and promised the same to every member of the army, wherever they were stationed.

The Senate

While it was still night, the consuls called the senate together in the temple of Jupiter the Conqueror. Deciding that liberty was a lost cause, many of the senators hid in the city instead of attending. Others left Rome and traveled to their farms, preferring to give up their positions and live quiet but safe lives as private citizens. All in all, only one hundred senators answered the summons.

While the senators discussed what should be done, the soldiers on their side suddenly grew impatient and demanded that the senate choose an emperor and give the government to one person, not to all. Still, there were those in the senate who were ambitious and wanted to rule. Marcus Minucianus was ready to claim the government himself. He was from an illustrious family and had married Julia, Caligula's sister, so he was a man of power, but the consuls discouraged him. Minucianus, who was also one of Caligula's murderers, likewise discouraged

Valerius of Asia from any hopes of power. A great slaughter would have occurred if these two men had been given permission to seek power for themselves and oppose Claudius, for the forces in Claudius's camp were growing every hour as gladiators, watchmen, and ships' rowers swelled his ranks.

As soon as it was light, Cherea and his followers came to the senate to speak to the soldiers there, but the soldiers refused to listen, demanding the senate stop delaying and choose a ruler. Cherea lost his temper and insulted the soldiers; in reply, they all left the senate and took an oath of loyalty to Claudius, leaving what was left of the senate defenseless and fearful for their lives.

People began flocking to Claudius's camp, eager to get on his good side now that he seemed destined to rule. Quintus Pomponius, one of the consuls, appeared. He would have been killed by the angry soldiers if Claudius had not saved him. The senators with Quintus did not fare as well; some received blows, and Aponius went away wounded. Only when Agrippa told Claudius to be more gentle with the senators he would have to rule did the soldiers cease threatening them.

The Conspirators

Claudius summoned the senate to the palace and was carried there himself through the city by the soldiers. Cherea and Sabinus, two of the conspirators, caused a stir by openly walking in front of the procession after they had been ordered not to appear in public by Pollio, Claudius's new captain of the guards. On reaching the palace, Claudius met with his friends to decide what should be done with the murderers. They all admitted Cherea had done a glorious deed, but in the end they decided he had to be killed to discourage such actions in the future.

Cherea and Lupus were led to their executions together. Cherea acted courageously, reproaching Lupus for crying like a coward and complaining of the cold when he took off his clothing. Cold, Cherea said, never hurt a lupus (wolf). When they reached the place of execution, Cherea asked his executioner if he was experienced in using his sword in this manner,

99

then requested to be killed with the sword he had used to kill Caligula. He died bravely, from one stroke. Lupus was not so fortunate, since he was too frightened to stretch out his neck; it took many blows to kill him.

A few days later, as all the Romans sacrificed during the Parental Solemnities, portions were put into the fire in honor of Cherea, and he was asked to forgive the Romans their ingratitude.

Sabinus was pardoned by Claudius and command of his army was returned to him, an outcome he felt was unjust to his fellow conspirators. He fell upon his own sword up to the hilt and killed himself.

SEVEN

As soon as Claudius had eliminated all the soldiers he distrusted, he published an edict reconfirming Agrippa's rule over all the land Caligula had given him and praising him highly. In addition, he enlarged Agrippa's kingdom to include all Judea and Samaria, which had once been ruled by Agrippa's grandfather, Herod the Great. Out of his own territory, Claudius gave Agrippa Abila of Lysanias and all the land that lay at Mount Libanus. Claudius then made a public league with Agrippa, confirmed by oaths, in the middle of Rome's forum.

Antiochus was relieved of his kingdom but given parts of Cilicia and Commagena. Claudius freed Alexander Lysimachus, his mother Antonia's steward and his old friend, who had been imprisoned by Caligula. Alexander's son Marcus had married Agrippa's daughter Bernice; when Marcus died, Agrippa gave Bernice in marriage to his brother Herod and asked Claudius to give Herod the kingdom of Chalcis.

As soon as Caligula was dead, trouble broke out between the Greeks and Jews living in the city of Alexandria. The Jews had been badly persecuted by the Greeks under Caligula's reign; now they had taken up arms to defend themselves. Claudius ordered the president of Egypt to restore order in Alexandria, then sent edicts to Alexandria and Syria at the urging of Agrippa and Herod. The edict sent to Alexandria proclaimed that the Jews should not be deprived of their ancient rights and privileges and were to be allowed to preserve their own customs and religion. The edict sent to the rest of the Roman Empire commanded that both the Jews and the Greeks were to be allowed to observe their own religions. The Jews were in turn to show respect for the religions of others in the empire.

Agrippa in Jerusalem

Agrippa was sent to rule his kingdom, which he was happy to do, returning to Jerusalem and offering all the sacrifices the Jewish law required of him. In strict observance of the laws, he ordered many of the Nazarites to shave their heads.

The golden chain that Caligula had given Agrippa on restoring his freedom was hung over the treasury of the temple in Jerusalem as a reminder that great men might fall and later regain their dignity. When Agrippa finished all the duties of worship, he removed Theophilus the son of Ananus from the high priesthood, giving it to Simon the son of Boethus, the father of one of Herod the Great's wives and a former high priest.

Grateful to the inhabitants of Jerusalem for the warm welcome they had given him, Agrippa relieved them from paying the tax on their houses. He also made Silas his general in recognition of his loyalty during the troubles they had shared.

Soon after Agrippa's return to Jerusalem, a Jewish synagogue was desecrated by some young men from the city of Doris, in Syria, who erected a statue of Caesar inside the synagogue. Agrippa went immediately to Publius Petronius, the president of Syria, and complained bitterly about this action. Petronius wrote to the magistrates of Doris and ordered the centurion Proculus Vitellius to bring the offenders to him for punishment, restating Caesar's orders that the Jews were to be allowed to practice their religion in peace.

Agrippa decided that Jonathan the son of Ananus was more worthy of the high priesthood than Simon, but Jonathan turned down the honor. Instead, he suggested Agrippa appoint his brother Matthias, who he said was pure from all sin against God and more worthy than he. Shortly after this, Marcus succeeded Petronius as president of Syria.

Silas

Silas, the new general of Agrippa's army, had been through much with Agrippa and had never hesitated to join him in any danger, but now he began to take advantage of Agrippa's friendship. He began to act as if he were Agrippa's equal, speaking freely on all occasions and constantly extolling his own bravery while reminding Agrippa of the hard times they had been through together. Men rarely like to be reminded of the times they were in shameful conditions, and only a foolish man constantly tells someone how kind he has been to him. Finally Agrippa had enough of Silas's boasting; he relieved him of his command, had him bound, and sent him back to prison in his own country.

But time eased Agrippa's anger toward Silas, who really had worked diligently for him over the years. When Agrippa celebrated his birthday by entertaining his subjects with a festival, he suddenly decided to send for Silas to be his guest.

Silas, always a frank man, told those who came for him that Agrippa was ungrateful and that he would never forgive him for his unfair mistreatment. He sent the messengers back, telling them to let Agrippa know exactly how he felt. Even then, Agrippa let Silas live.

Agrippa's Works

Agrippa began repairing the walls of Jerusalem that adjoined the new city (Bezetha), building them wider and higher. They would have been too strong for anyone to destroy if Marcus, the president of Syria, had not told Claudius what Agrippa was doing. Claudius, thinking Agrippa might be planning to revolt, ordered the building stopped.

Agrippa was naturally a very generous man who enjoyed a good reputation. He was nothing like the Herod who reigned before him, who was ill-natured, cruel, and more interested in the Greeks than in the Jews. Agrippa was mild-mannered and generous to all, even foreigners. He lived in the city of Jerusalem, observing the laws and keeping himself entirely pure.

Once when the king was in Cesarea, Simon, a man very learned in the law, accused Agrippa of not living a holy life. He claimed that Agrippa could justly be excluded from the temple, since it only belonged to native Jews.

Agrippa's general reported this speech to Agrippa, who sent for Simon and received him in the theater. Agrippa told Simon to sit down beside him and then quietly asked, "What is done here that is contrary to the law?" Simon, who could find no answer, begged Agrippa's forgiveness. Preferring mildness to anger and moderation to passion, Agrippa gave Simon a small present and dismissed him.

Agrippa was a great builder in many towns, but especially in Berytus, where he built a great theater, an amphitheater, baths, and porticoes at great expense. For the dedication of these buildings, he brought in shows and musicians of all sorts. He also showed his magnificence at the theater when he brought in 1,400 men as gladiators — all the prisoners he had — and had them all destroyed at once.

When the work at Berytus was completed, Agrippa moved to Tiberias, in Galilee. The other kings of the area regarded him highly, and many of them came there to visit him: Antiochus, the king of Commagena; Sampsigeramus, king of Emesa; Cotys, king of Lesser Armenia; Polemo, king of Pontus; and Agrippa's brother Herod, king of Chalcis. All these he entertained royally in return for the respect they showed him by their visits.

While the kings were staying with Agrippa, Marcus, the president of Syria, came to town. To show his respect for the Romans, Agrippa went out to meet Marcus about a mile from town, bringing his other guests with him. As a Roman official, Marcus did not think it was a good sign that all these local kings were so friendly with one another; he sent his servants to each king and ordered them all home immediately, which instantly made him Agrippa's enemy.

About this time, Agrippa took the high priesthood away from Matthias and gave it to Elioneus the son of Cantheras.

Agrippa's Death

When Agrippa had reigned three years over all Judea (A.D. 44), he went to Cesarea to present shows in honor of Caesar. A great crowd had assembled for the shows, including the most prominent people in the province. On the second day of the shows, Agrippa dressed himself in a beautifully made garment of silver and went to the theater early in the morning, when the rising sun reflected off his garment, stunning the crowd with its brightness. Soon voices began to call out from the crowd, proclaiming Agrippa a god and asking for his mercy.

Agrippa did not reject the crowd's impious flattery or rebuke them at this point, but on looking up, he saw an owl sitting on a rope over his head. He knew immediately that the bird was a messenger of bad news, as once before it had been a messenger of good news. A severe pain suddenly arose in his belly. Agrippa looked at his friends and informed them he was going to die soon. God was reproving their lying words, he said; he was not an immortal god. But he accepted God's will on this matter because he had lived a happy life. As he finished speaking, his pain increased and he was carried to the palace.

Word went out that Agrippa was dying. As required by law, the crowds sat in sackcloth with their wives and children, beseeching God for their king's recovery; every place was filled with mourning.

Agrippa, resting in a high chamber, looked down at the mourning crowds lying prostrate on the ground and wept. At the end of five days, he died at the age of fifty-four, after reigning seven years. He reigned four years under Caligula, three of them over Philip's tetrarchy and the fourth over Philip's and Herod's. In addition to those years, he reigned over Judea, Samaria, Cesarea, and his other lands for three years under Claudius. The revenues he received were no less than 12 million drachmae, yet he borrowed great sums from others because he was so generous that his expenses were greater than his income.

Before the crowds were told of Agrippa's death, Herod, the king of Chalcis, and Helcias, Agrippa's general, sent Aristo, one of Agrippa's most faithful servants, to kill Silas, so it would appear it had been done on Agrippa's orders.

After Agrippa's Death

On his death, Agrippa left behind a seventeen-year-old son named Agrippa and three daughters. Bernice, sixteen, was married to Agrippa's brother Herod; Mariamne was ten; Drusilla, six. Before he died, Agrippa had engaged his two unmarried daughters. Mariamne was to marry Julius Archelaus Epiphanes, the son of Antiochus, who was the son of Chalcias. Drusilla was engaged to the king of Commagena.

Once it was known that Agrippa was dead, the people of Cesarea and Sebaste forgot his kindness to them and acted as though they were his enemies, rejoicing in his death and slandering his name. A great number of soldiers stationed in these cities went to Agrippa's house and carried off the statues of Agrippa's daughters. (Some sources say they actually took the girls, not their statues.) They took the statues to the tops of the brothels, abused them terribly, and committed indecent acts with them. The soldiers also put garlands on their own heads and celebrated Agrippa's death with ointments, feasts, and toasts to Charon. Not only were they desecrating the memory of Agrippa, who had been more than generous to them, but also that of Herod the Great, who had spent vast sums of money rebuilding and improving both Cesarea and Sebaste.

Agrippa's son was in Rome, being brought up by Claudius Caesar. On hearing of Agrippa's death, Claudius first thought to send Agrippa II back to rule in his father's place, but his advisers convinced him the boy was too young and inexperienced to rule such a large kingdom. Claudius knew that Agrippa and Marcus, the president of Syria, had been enemies, so he refrained from giving Marcus control of the kingdom and sent Cuspius Fadus to serve as procurator of Judea and the rest of Agrippa's kingdom. He sent Fadus orders to punish the inhabitants of Cesarea and Sebaste for their actions and to transfer the five regiments there to Pontus, replacing them with soldiers stationed in Syria. The transfer never took place, however; the soldiers sent ambassadors to Claudius and convinced him to change his mind. These same soldiers would later cause the Jews great suffering and sow the seeds of Jewish revolt.

Many times while he was alive, Agrippa had written to Claudius asking him to replace Marcus as president of Syria. Out of respect for Agrippa's memory, Claudius now replaced Marcus with Cassius Longinus.

As soon as Fadus arrived in Judea, he was greeted by problems between the Jews of Perea and the people of Philadelphia, who were arguing about the border at a village called Mia. The Jews of Perea, without the consent of their leaders, had proceeded to arm themselves and kill many Philadelphians, which angered Fadus, who thought they should have come to him for justice. Fadus had three of the Jewish leaders arrested; Hannibal was executed, while Amram and Eleazar were banished.

A little while later Tholomy, a notorious bandit, was captured and slain, but not before he had caused a great deal of trouble in Idumea and Arabia. From then on, Fadus kept Judea free of bandits.

Fadus now sent for the high priest and leaders of Jerusalem and told them that the high priest's vestments should be surrendered to Roman protection. The Jews asked permission to send ambassadors to Claudius, in hopes he would let them keep the vestments themselves. Second, they asked that nothing be done until Claudius's reply was received. The ambassadors were allowed to go to Rome when the Jewish leaders turned their sons over to the Romans as pledges of peaceful behavior. When the ambassadors arrived in Rome, young Agrippa asked Claudius to grant their request, which he did, telling the ambassadors they had Agrippa to thank for his decision.

Herod, the king of Chalcis, who was Agrippa the First's brother, now petitioned Caesar for control of the temple, the sacred treasure, and the authority to choose the high priest, obtaining all he asked for. Herod then removed Cantheras from office and appointed Joseph the son of Camus high priest.

Helena and Izates

Some years ago, Monobazus Bazeus, the king of Adiabene, fell in love with his sister Helena and married her. In bed with her one night when she was pregnant, Monobazus fell asleep with his hand on his wife's belly, then thought he heard a voice telling him to remove his hands from her and be careful not to hurt the child she was carrying. The child, he heard, would be born safely and have a good life.

When the baby was born, Monobazus named him Izates. Although he and Helena had an older son named Monobazus and the king had other sons by other wives, he so openly favored Izates that his other children became jealous and hated the boy. Their father understood how the older children felt and forgave them their hatred, but to keep Izates safe, he sent him to Abennerig, the king of Charax-Spasini, to be raised in safety. Abennerig welcomed the boy into his family, married him to his daughter Samacha, and gave him one of his countries to rule, from which Izates received large revenues.

Monobazus grew old and realized he had a limited time left to live. He wanted to see Izates one more time, so he sent for him and gave him the country of Carrae, a country rich in amomum that also contained the remains of Noah's ark. Izates lived in Carrae until Monobazus's death.

On the day of Monobazus's death, Helena sent for all the nobles and governors of the kingdom. Monobazus had intended that Izates inherit the kingdom, she told them, but she wanted to know how they felt about that, believing it best for a ruler if he had the support of those he would rule. Her advisers wholeheartedly approved of Izates and urged Helena to have all his brothers killed for the sake of his safety. Helena would not agree to that without Izates's approval, but she was convinced to have the brothers bound until Izates could reach Adiabene and claim the kingdom. In the meantime, her eldest son, Monobazus, would serve as the temporary ruler.

While Izates had lived in Charax-Spasini, both he and his mother had separately converted to Judaism. Arriving in Adiabene to assume the throne, Izates found his brothers in

108

prison. He believed it would be impious to keep them imprisoned or execute them, yet they would be a danger to him if they were set free, so he sent some of them to Claudius as hostages and others to Artabanus, the king of Parthia.

Once Izates discovered that Helena had also converted to Judaism, he totally embraced the Jewish customs and decided to be circumcised. Helena discouraged this, saying his subjects would not support a king who openly followed a foreign religion; circumcision would endanger his life. Even Izates's Jewish teacher, Ananias, advised against his circumcision. He could worship God without that, he said; God would understand that circumcision was too dangerous for Izates. For the time being, Izates followed their advice, but later, at the urging of Eleazer of Galilee, he went ahead with his plan and was circumcised.

Once Helena saw that her son was safe and the affairs of the country were running smoothly, she asked Izates's permission to travel to Jerusalem and worship at the temple. Izates agreed and provided her with a great deal of money for the trip. Helena arrived in Jerusalem during a great famine (A.D. 46 -48), which was causing many deaths. She immediately sent servants to Alexandria to buy large amounts of wheat and to Cyprus to buy a cargo of dried figs, then distributed the food to those in need. Izates also supplied a large amount of money to the leaders of Jerusalem to help relieve the famine.

Artabanus

Artabanus, king of the Parthians, now discovered that the governors of his provinces were planning to kill him. Deciding it wasn't safe to remain in Parthia, he fled to Izates for help, taking a thousand of his family and servants with him. Izates knew of Artabanus, but the two had never met, so when they met on the road, Izates didn't recognize the king. Artabanus, with tears in his eyes, begged for help in regaining his kingdom. As soon as Izates realized who Artabanus was, he treated him with all honor and agreed to help him.

Izates wrote to the Parthians, urging them to accept Artabanus as their king again. Although they didn't refuse, they said they had already appointed Cinnamus king and feared a civil war if Artabanus were to return. Cinnamus, who had been brought up by Artabanus, was a good, gentle man; he wrote to Artabanus himself, telling him to return and take over the throne, which he would willingly surrender.

In gratitude to Izates, Artabanus bestowed on him the highest Parthian honors and gave him the country of Nisibis, which contained the city called Antioch of Mygodonia.

Shortly thereafter, Artabanus died, leaving his kingdom to his son Bardanes, who tried to convince Izates to join him in a revolt against the Romans. Izates refused, and Bardanes was killed by his countrymen, to be succeeded by his brother Gotarzes, who was also soon killed. Another brother, Vologases, became king of Parthia, turning over the province of Medes to one of his brothers, Pacorus, and Armenia to another brother, Tiridates.

Izates the King

When Izates's older brother, Monobazus, and the rest of his family saw how Izates's piety had brought him great esteem in the eyes of men, they also converted to Judaism. This displeased the nobles of Adiabene, who wrote to Abia, king of the Arabians, and offered him a large amount of money to attack Izates. They would desert Izates as soon as the battle began, they assured him.

At the beginning of the battle, the nobles all pretended to panic and ran off, which didn't bother Izates too much until he learned their panic was actually desertion. He killed the conspiring nobles he caught, then returned to defeat Abia's army on the following day, driving its survivors into the fortress of Arsamus, which he besieged and took, then plundered. Abia killed himself when he saw he was defeated.

Even though their first attempt had failed, the remaining nobles tried again. They contacted Vologases, the king of Parthia, asking him to kill Izates and give them a Parthian ruler instead of one who had embraced a foreign religion. Vologases had no justification for making war on Izates, so he demanded

Izates give up the Parthian honors bestowed on him by his father, knowing Izates would refuse and thus provide an excuse for war.

Izates realized that giving in to Vologases's demands would not prevent a war; Vologases would simply find another excuse. He put his wives and children in a strong fortress, stocked all his fortresses with a good supply of wheat, then burned the grass and hay and waited for the Parthians.

Vologases arrived with a great army and built an earthen fortification on the bank of the river that divided Adiabene from Media. Izates and his army of six thousand horsemen camped nearby. Then a messenger arrived from Vologases to tell Izates how big the Parthian kingdom was — stretching from the Euphrates to Bactria — and how many subjects Vologases commanded. Vologases had come to punish Izates for his ingratitude, and no god could save him.

Izates replied that he was well aware of Vologases's superior power; but his God was more powerful than any man. When the messengers left with his answer, Izates made supplication to God, throwing himself on the ground, putting ashes on his head, and fasting with his family. Then he prayed, asking God's help not only for himself, but for His own honor.

That night Vologases received news that the Dahae and Sacae, who hated him, were attacking Parthia in his absence and laying it waste; Vologases retired to defend his own kingdom. Thus did Izates escape war with the Parthians through the providence of God.

Shortly after this, Izates died at the age of fifty-five, having ruled twenty-four years. He left behind him twenty-four sons and twenty-four daughters, but left the kingdom to his older brother, Monobazus, in repayment for his having faithfully preserved the kingdom after their father's death.

Helena, mourning the death of Izates but happy that her elder son would rule in his place, returned to Adiabene to be with him and died shortly after arriving. Monobazus sent the bones of Helena and Izates to Jerusalem for burial in the three pyramids Helena had built there less than a half mile from the city.

EIGHT

While Fadus was procurator of Judea (A.D. 45 or 46), a magician named Theudas persuaded a large number of Jews to take their possessions and follow him to the river Jordan. He claimed to be a prophet and promised to divide the river, allowing them easy passage across it. Fadus sent a troop of horsemen out to prevent this attempt; they killed many of the Jews and captured many alive, cutting off Theudas's head and taking it back with them to Jerusalem.

Fadus was succeeded by Tiberius Alexander as procurator. It was under these procurators that the great famine hit Judea and Queen Helena imported wheat from Egypt to feed the starving. Also during this period James and Simon, the sons of Judas of Galilee, who had raised a revolt during Cyrenius's taxation, were crucified by Alexander. Herod, king of Chalcis, removed Joseph, son of Camydus, from the high priesthood and gave the office to Ananias, the son of Nebedeus.

Tiberius Alexander was replaced as procurator by Cumanus, and Herod, Agrippa the First's brother, died (A.D. 49). Herod left behind Aristobulus, his son by his first wife, and Bernicianus and Hyrcanus by his wife Bernice, who was also his niece. Claudius gave Herod's kingdom to Agrippa II.

A great tragedy then befell the Jews during the reign of Cumanus at one of the Passover feasts. A large number of Jews had come to Jerusalem to celebrate the feast, which made Cumanus nervous about the possibility of revolt. As former procurators had always done, Cumanus stationed a regiment of soldiers in the temple cloister as a preventative measure. On the fourth day of the feast, one of the Roman soldiers dropped his pants and exposed himself to the crowd in the temple.

The Jews saw the soldier's action as an insult not only to themselves, but to God, and accused Cumanus of arranging the incident. When he was not able to quiet the crowd, Cumanus ordered the whole army to occupy the tower of Antonia, which overlooked the temple. The crowd panicked, and at least 20,000 Jews died in the crush that ensued.

Shortly after this, some of the Jews traveling on the road about twelve and a half miles from Jerusalem robbed Stephanus, one of Caesar's servants. Hearing of the robbery, Cumanus immediately sent soldiers to plunder the villages nearby and take their leaders captive. As the plundering was going on, one of the soldiers found and willfully destroyed one of the villages' Laws of Moses. When the Jews heard of this, a great number of them traveled to Cumanus in Cesarea, demanding he avenge this affront to God. On advice of his friends, Cumanus had the offending soldier beheaded, thus quieting the Jews.

The Samaritans and the Jews

Galileans traveling to Jerusalem for festivals normally passed through Samaria on their trip. Along their path on the great plain lay a Samaritan village named Ginea, whose inhabitants attacked and killed many Galileans as they passed through one day.

Hearing of the attack, the Galilean leaders went to Cumanus to urge him to avenge this murder of their people. However, Cumanus had been bribed by the Samaritans and refused the Galileans' petition. Some Galileans then encouraged all the Jews to take up arms and revolt, saying it was bad enough to

114

live in slavery, but slavery combined with murder was unbearable. Combining forces with Eleazar, a robber living in the mountains, they proceeded to plunder many Samaritan villages despite the efforts of the Jewish leaders to prevent their actions.

When Cumanus heard of this, he took the army from Sebaste, with four regiments of foot soldiers, armed the Samaritans, and killed many of the rebellious Jews. As soon as they saw how far things had gone, the leaders of the Jews in Jerusalem put on sackcloth, poured ashes on their heads, and entreated the rebels to stop their attacks on Samaria before the whole country was destroyed, the temple burned, and all the Jews thrown into slavery. This time the people listened to their leaders and dispersed. The bandits returned to the mountains, from where they soon tormented all of Judea with their robberies.

Now the Samaritan leaders traveled to Tyre to see Ummidius Quadratus, the Roman president of Syria, complaining that the Jews were plundering their villages. This showed great disrespect for the Romans, the Samaritans said. If the Jews felt they had been injured, why hadn't they first gone to the Romans for justice?

On their part, the Jews maintained the problem had been started by the Samaritans and ignored by Cumanus because he was bribed. Quadratus tended to believe the Jews, but held off making a decision until he had time to investigate.

Soon after, Quadratus traveled to Judea. Hearing the Jews were still rebellious, he ordered the crucifixion of those that had been taken captive by Cumanus, then traveled to Lydda to hear both sides again. He ordered Dortus and four other Jewish rebel leaders killed, then sent Ananias, the high priest, and Ananus, the commander of the temple, in bonds to Rome for Claudius's decision. In addition, he sent the leaders of both sides, Cumanus, and Celer the tribune, to the emperor. Returning to Jerusalem, Quadratus found the city peaceful and left for Antioch.

Because Caesar's freedmen and friends were on their side, Cumanus and the Samaritan leaders would have easily won their argument before Claudius if not for Agrippa II, who was in Rome at that time. Agrippa begged Claudius's wife, Agrippina, to see that Claudius judged the case fairly. Claudius decided the Samaritans had started the whole problem; their ambassadors were executed, and Cumanus was banished. Celer the tribune was taken to Jerusalem, drawn through the city, and executed.

Agrippa's Family

Claudius sent Felix, the brother of Pallans, to take over the affairs of Judea as procurator (A.D. 52), and at the end of his twelfth year as Caesar (A.D. 53), he gave Agrippa II Philip's tetrarchy plus Batanea, Trachonitis, and Abila (the former tetrarchy of Lysanius). At the same time, he took Chalcis away from Agrippa II after he had governed it for four years.

Agrippa II gave his sister Drusilla in marriage to Azizus, the king of Emesa, after Azizus agreed to be circumcised. Although she had been promised to Epiphanes, he had refused to accept the Jewish faith as he had promised Agrippa I he would. Agrippa's second sister, Mariamne, married the man her father had chosen for her: Archelaus, the son of Helcias. Mariamne and Archelaus had a daughter named Bernice.

Felix the procurator soon saw Drusilla and fell in love with her, for she was more beautiful than any other woman he knew. He sent a Cypriot Jew named Simon to speak to Drusilla for him. Simon, pretending to be a magician, promised Drusilla he could make her a happy woman if she would divorce Azizus and marry Felix, which she did. She and Felix had a son named Agrippa, who later perished with his wife during an eruption of Vesuvius.

Bernice, Agrippa the Second's third sister, lived a long time as a widow after the death of her husband, Herod, the king of Chalcis — who was both her husband and her uncle. But when rumors began circulating that she was having sexual relations with her brother, she persuaded Polemo, the king of Cilicia, to be circumcised and marry her, hoping the marriage would stop the rumors. Polemo agreed, mainly because of Bernice's wealth, but Bernice soon divorced him to pursue other men, and Polemo renounced the Jewish faith.

At the same time, Mariamne divorced Archelaus to marry Demetrius, the wealthy alabarch of the Alexandrian Jews; they had a son named Agrippinus.

The Death of Claudius

After a reign of thirteen years, eight months, and twenty days (October 13, 54), Claudius died, probably poisoned by his wife, Agrippina.

Agrippina's father had been Germanicus, Claudius's brother. She was previously married to Domitius Aenobarbus, one of Rome's most illustrious citizens, and married Claudius some years after her first husband's death. When she and Claudius married, Agrippina brought along a son from her first marriage, who was named Domitius after his father and later changed his name to Nero on being adopted by Claudius.

Before his marriage to Agrippina, Claudius had killed his second wife, Messalina, out of jealousy. They had two children: Britannicus and Octavia. By his first wife, Pelina, Claudius had a daughter named Antonia. Claudius married Nero to his daughter Octavia.

To assure that Nero would succeed on Claudius's death instead of Britannicus, Agrippina poisoned Claudius. She then arranged to have Burrhus (the general of the army), the tribunes, and the highest-ranking freedmen take Nero into camp and proclaim him emperor.

As soon as Nero obtained control of the government, he secretly had Britannicus poisoned and publicly executed his mother, his wife, and many other high-ranking people for plotting against him.

The Assassins

In the first year of Nero's reign Azizus, the king of Emesa, died; his brother Soemus succeeded him. Aristobulus, the son of Herod the king of Chalcis, was given control of Lesser

Armenia. Agrippa II was given parts of Galilee, Tiberias, Taricheae, the city of Julias in Perea, and fourteen cities around Julias.

The affairs of the Jews were growing more troubled. The country was filled with robbers and false prophets fooling the people, although Felix was successful in capturing and killing many of them, including the robber Eleazar.

Felix hated the high priest, Jonathan, who persisted in telling him how to run the country, and devised a plot to have him killed. He persuaded Doras, one of Jonathan's best friends, to arrange to have Jonathan killed by bribing some robbers to do the job. The robbers came into the city as if they were going to worship, daggers hidden under their clothing. Mingling with the crowd, they were able to murder the high priest and escape safely. Since they were not caught and punished, the robbers (named sicarii for the short, curved swords they carried) returned again and again to murder others in the city and in the temple itself — their own enemies and those whom they were paid to kill — not at all concerned about the sacrilege of such murders.

And this seems to be the reason God rejected Jerusalem and its impure temple and brought the Romans upon the Jews, purging the city with fire and sending the Jews into slavery as a lesson to them.

Jerusalem filled with impiety. Deceivers and false prophets arose, leading the Jews into the wilderness in search of signs and wonders from God. Many that went with them were brought back and punished by Felix. One of these imposters came out of Egypt and convinced a multitude of common people to follow him to the Mount of Olives, promising them the walls of Jerusalem would fall at his command. Hearing these claims, Felix sent his soldiers against the Egyptian and his followers; 400 were killed and 200 captured, but the Egyptian escaped.

Again the robbers encouraged the people to disobey the Romans; those who would not comply with them had their villages burned and plundered.

At this time trouble broke out between the Jews and the Syrians dwelling in Cesarea over which group was the most prominent in the city. When Felix attempted to stop the fighting, the Jews refused to listen to him, so he sent his soldiers out to restore peace, killing many Jews and plundering their houses until the Jewish leaders convinced him to call in his troops.

Now Agrippa II gave the high priesthood to Ismael the son of Fabi, and conflict broke out between the high priests of the temple and the leaders of Jerusalem. Both sides collected supporters and fought each other with words and stones until the city was reduced to lawlessness. When the high priests of the temple sent servants to the threshing floors to take all the tithes due all the priests, a great number of local priests died from starvation.

Porcius Festus replaced Felix as procurator (A.D. 60) and the Jewish leaders of Cesarea traveled to Rome to accuse Felix. He would certainly have been punished for his actions in Judea if it were not for the intervention of Nero's brother Pallas.

Two of the leaders of the Syrians in Cesarea then bribed Burrhus, who was Nero's tutor, to convince Nero to rescind the equality of the Jews living in Cesarea. Nero allowed Burrhus to write a letter doing just that, which would eventually lead to a Jewish rebellion when the Jews of Cesarea were informed of the letter's contents.

About the same time, Agrippa II built himself a dining room in the royal palace of Jerusalem, from which he could easily look down into the temple itself. This displeased the Jewish leaders, who erected a wall that not only blocked the king's view of the sacrifices but also of the cloisters where the Roman guards stood during the festivals. Festus ordered the wall destroyed but held off acting until the Jews could send ambassadors for Nero's ruling on the matter. When Nero heard the ambassadors, he allowed the wall to stand, mainly in order to please his wife, Poppea, who was a religious woman. He sent the ambassadors home, keeping Helcias, the keeper of the sacred treasure, and Ismael, the high priest, as hostages. Agrippa II replaced Ismael with Joseph Cabi, the son of Simon.

119

Albinus and Agrippa II

On the death of Festus (A.D. 62), Nero sent Albinus to Judea as procurator. Agrippa II took the high priesthood away from Joseph and gave it to the son of Ananus, who was also named Ananus. The elder Ananus had been high priest himself many years ago and had five sons, all of whom served in that office, which had never happened before.

The young Ananus was very insolent and bold, a strict Sadduccee who took advantage of the fact that there was no procurator in Judea, since Albinus had not yet arrived. He assembled the sanhedrim and brought James, the brother of Jesus Christ, before them, accusing him and those with him of breaking the law and ordering them stoned (although they were not killed).

This action was against Roman law, which required that the procurator must give consent for the sanhedrim to assemble, and many citizens disliked what was done. Word was sent to Agrippa II and Albinus, informing them of what Ananus had done and asking that he be restrained. Albinus promised to punish Ananas; Agrippa II took the high priesthood from him after only three months and made Jesus, the son of Damneus, high priest.

A former high priest named Ananias (Annas or Annanus the Elder) living in Jerusalem became more and more powerful each day due to the respect the citizens had for him and his great riches. By giving them gifts, Ananias cultivated the friendship of Albinus and the high priest, Jesus. He and the other high priests sent their servants to the threshing floors and took by force the tithes that belonged to all the priests, so some of the priests that were deprived of their living starved to death.

One night before the festival, the sicarii came into the city and kidnapped Eleazar, Ananias's son, holding him captive until Ananias convinced Albinus to release ten sicarii captives. This was the beginning of further problems, for the sicarii continued to capture Ananias's servants and so freed more and more sicarii, until they afflicted the whole country.

About this time Agrippa II enlarged Cesarea Philippi and

renamed it Neronias. He built an expensive theater in Berytus and arranged yearly shows there at great cost, gave the people large supplies of wheat and oil, and decorated the city with art from all over the kingdom. By spending so much on this foreign city and depriving his own people, Agrippa II earned their hatred.

Jesus the son of Gamaliel replaced Jesus the son of Damneus as high priest, which caused a conflict among the high priests, who gathered bands of men together to fight one another with stones. Because of his great wealth, Ananias was stronger than all the rest. Costobarus and Saulus, members of the royal family, also gathered supporters and plundered those weaker than themselves. All of Jerusalem was now in a state of disorder.

Hearing that Gessius Florus was on his way to succeed him as procurator, Albinus cleaned out his prisons, killing the worst offenders and accepting bribes for the release of those imprisoned on minor charges, thus releasing more criminals into the countryside.

Those Levites who were hymn singers now convinced Agrippa II to assemble a sanhedrim and give them permission to wear the linen garments worn by priests; other Levites serving in the temple were allowed to study to become hymn singers. All of this was against Jewish law.

It was now decided to finish the building of the temple courts, a project that required over 18,000 imported workmen and put many local Jews who had been working in the temple out of work. To support themselves, the Jews of Jerusalem requested Agrippa's permission to rebuild the eastern cloisters. The foundation of the cloisters was in a deep valley: their walls were six hundred feet high, built of white stones thirty feet long and nine feet high. Agrippa turned down their request because of the time and money involved but allowed them to pave the city streets with white stone. He also took the high priesthood away from Jesus the son of Gamaliel and gave it to Matthias the son of Theophilus.

The High Priests

Aaron, the brother of Moses, served as the first Jewish high

121

priest, and after his death was succeeded by his sons, from which came the law that only those related to Aaron by blood could serve as high priest. Thirteen high priests descended from Aaron served for the 612 years between the departure from Egypt and the building of Solomon's temple. After them, eighteen served in Jerusalem for a total of 466 years, 6 months, and 10 days, until Nebuchadnezzar took the Jews as captives to Babylonia.

After 70 years of captivity, Cyrus allowed the Jews to return to their own land, and Jesus the son of Josadek took the high priesthood. He and his successors, a total of 15 high priests, served for 414 years.

At the end of this time, Jacimus was high priest for three years, but no one succeeded him, and the city had no priest for the next seven years. Jonathan was then appointed and served seven years, followed by Simon and Hyrcanus, who held the office for thirty years. Aristobulus succeeded Hyrcanus for one year; he was succeeded as king and priest by his brother Alexander, who ruled twenty-seven years.

The next high priest was Hyrcanus, who was high priest for nine years before his brother Aristobulus defeated him and reigned for three years and three months. Pompey restored the office to Hyrcanus, who ruled twenty-four additional years. Antigonus reigned three years and three months. Herod made Aristobulus the next high priest, but killed him the following year. The number of high priests from the time of Herod until the burning of the temple was twenty-eight; they served for a total of one hundred and seven years.

NINE

Gessius Florus succeeded Albinus as procurator (A.D. 64) and made Albinus almost seem decent by comparison, for while Albinus was secretive about his evil deeds, Florus made no attempts to appear just. Florus did not think it worth his while to rob individuals; he spoiled whole cities at once, giving total freedom to any robbers who split their profits with him. Under Florus, entire toparchies were desolated and a great number of people fled to other countries.

Cestius Gallus was now president of Syria. Although no one had dared complain to him about Florus before, over 3 million Jews approached him when he came to Jerusalem to celebrate the Passover (A.D. 65), complaining that Florus was destroying their country. Florus, who was present at this accusation, laughed at the charges. Cestius quieted the crowd and assured them Florus would treat them more gently in the future; Florus assured Cestius he would mend his ways.

In truth, Florus was afraid the Jews would bring charges against him before Caesar and all his illegal acts would come to light. The only thing that could prevent that was an outright revolt of the Jews. Florus made their lives worse than ever, hoping to induce them to rebel.

Cesarea

The Jewish revolt began in A.D. 66 in the city of Cesarea after the Greeks were given control of the government by Nero. The Jews of the city had their synagogue on property owned by a Cesarean Greek. Although they had offered to buy it from the Greek at many times its value, he refused to sell and began to build upon the land. The leaders of the Cesarean Jews and John the publican bribed Florus with eight talents to stop the work around the synagogue; Florus took the money and promptly left for Sebaste, as though giving the Jews permission to use force.

The following day, as the Jews went to the synagogue to worship, a man from Cesarea set an earthen vessel upside down at the entrance of the synagogue and sacrificed birds on it, which was part of the Jewish ritual of cleansing a leper and therefore insulted the Jews as a leprous people. The more moderate Jews urged going to the governors about the insult. The younger Jews were ready to fight and found more than willing Greeks close at hand.

Jucundus, the Roman officer in charge, took away the earthen vessel and attempted to restore order, but he was not able to do so. The Jews collected their books of the law and retired to Narbata, one of their villages about seven and a half miles from Cesarea. John and twelve other Jewish leaders went to Florus in Sebaste to ask for help, reminding him of the eight talents they had given him; Florus threw them in prison for removing the books of the law from Cesarea.

Jerusalem

Although the Jews of Jerusalem were outraged at the events in Cesarea, they kept their peace until Florus removed seventeen talents from the sacred treasure, claiming Caesar wanted them. Then they went to the temple, calling on Caesar for assistance and reproaching Florus. Some even carried baskets through the crowd as if collecting money for a destitute person, in order to shame Florus.

Instead of going to Cesarea to restore peace as he should

have, Florus marched on Jerusalem with a Roman army. The people of Jerusalem, hoping to shame him, went out to meet the army with all courtesy, planning to acclaim Florus and play the part of submissive subjects, but Florus sent Capito, a centurion, ahead of him with fifty soldiers and a message telling the Jews to stop their pretending. If they wanted to make fun of him, they should do so to his face, not only with words but with weapons. Capito's horsemen dispersed the crowd before it could shame Florus.

The next day Florus set up court in the palace, calling the high priest and leaders to it and demanding they surrender those who had tried to insult him the day before. The Jewish leaders apologized for the crowd's actions, saying it was impossible to separate the guilty from the innocent in such a crowd, but that everyone was sorry for what had happened.

Provoked by the response, Florus called out to his soldiers, ordering them to go plunder the upper marketplace and kill anyone they met there, which they did with thoroughness and greed. Many of the innocent people captured by the troops were whipped and crucified; the total number of men, women, and children killed that day was 3,600.

On that day, Florus did what no one had ever done before: He ordered Jews serving in the civil service, who were legal Roman citizens, whipped and crucified, an act prohibited by Roman law.

Bernice

At this time Bernice, King Agrippa's sister, was living in Jerusalem in order to perform a vow she had made to God that required her to sacrifice for thirty days, abstain from wine, and shave her head. She was greatly upset by the actions of the soldiers and sent the masters of her horse and guards to Florus to beg him to stop the slaughter. He would not comply with her request.

Bernice went to Florus herself and stood before him barefooted to ask him to spare the Jews. He paid her no respect at all; indeed, his soldiers would have killed her if she hadn't fled to the palace.

The Roman Troops

The day after the slaughter, the crowd gathered at the upper marketplace to mourn their dead and accuse Florus, but their leaders convinced them to return to their homes and avoid further deaths.

But Florus wanted the rebellion to continue, not end. He called the Jewish leaders to him, telling them the only way they could prove their peaceful intentions was to go greet the two cohorts of soldiers coming in from Cesarea. At the same time, he ordered the approaching soldiers not to return the Jews' salutations. If the Jews complained about Florus, he said the soldiers should use their weapons.

The high priests assembled the crowd in the temple and appeared before them in mourning, carrying the holy vessels and their ornamental garments and encouraging the people to greet the Romans politely. If they did so, the priests said, Florus would have no cause to begin a war with them.

In this way, they quieted the seditious and won the crowd to their point of view, leading them out to greet the approaching soldiers, which they did with respect. When the soldiers refused to return their greetings, some of the seditious in the crowd called out against Florus, and the Romans attacked the crowd as ordered, killing many and causing a panic that crushed even more. The crowd was pushed through Bezetha as the soldiers forced their way through to take the tower of Antonia and the temple.

Florus was also eager to take Antonia and the temple's treasure. He led his soldiers out of the palace, but the crowd turned on them and threw darts down at them from the rooftops, forcing the soldiers to retreat to the palace.

Some of the Jews, afraid Florus would return and capture the temple, climbed to the top of the cloisters adjoining Antonia and knocked them down. Although Florus was eager to capture the temple treasure, he stopped his attempts once the cloisters were destroyed. He called together the high priests and the sanhedrim and told them he was leaving the city but would leave troops behind to help them maintain the peace. The

Jewish leaders promised there would be no trouble as long as the soldiers left were not those who had fought the Jews. Florus gave them the soldiers they requested and took the rest of his army to Cesarea.

Still looking for a way to make the Jews rebel, Florus wrote to Cestius, accusing them of revolution against the Roman government. The leaders of Jerusalem and Bernice also sent letters to Cestius about Florus. In order to find out the true facts of the matter, Cestius sent a tribune named Neopolitanus to meet Agrippa at Jamnia and look into the problem with him.

The high priests and sanhedrim, along with other Jewish leaders, paid their respects to Agrippa and informed him of Florus's brutality. Florus's actions angered Agrippa, but he didn't show his feelings to the Jewish delegation. Instead, he made light of their complaints, even turning some of their complaints against them in hopes of preventing them from seeking vengeance.

The citizens of Jerusalem met Agrippa and Neopolitanus five miles from town, mourning and lamenting, begging the two men to help them. When they arrived in the city, the crowd showed them the desolation of the marketplace and the plundered houses, convincing Neopolitanus to inspect the city for himself and see how the Jews were submissive to all Romans except Florus. When he finished his tour, Neopolitanus called them all to the temple to commend them for their loyalty to the Romans and urge them to keep the peace. Following that, he returned to report to Cestius.

Agrippa's Speech

The crowd asked Agrippa and the high priests for permission to send ambassadors to Nero. Agrippa thought that would be extremely dangerous, yet the crowd was in a warlike mood. He called them all together, placed his sister Bernice where she could be seen by all, and spoke to them.

Agrippa asked why the Jews were so eager to go to war against the Roman Empire. To avenge the wrongs they had suffered from one man? Rome itself had not hurt them — Rome didn't even know of Florus's actions. Soon a new procurator would be appointed, and perhaps their wrongs would be righted. Or did they seek to regain their liberty? It was too late for that once Pompey took Jerusalem. Far stronger people than they had submitted to Roman rule once they were defeated, and they now lived with very few Roman soldiers in their midst. "You are the only people who think it a disgrace to be servants to those to whom all the world hath submitted."

What sort of army did they have? Where were their arms, their fleet, the riches they would need? "Are you richer than the Gauls, stronger than the Germans, wiser than the Greeks, more numerous than all men upon this habitable earth?" the king asked.

Yes, it's hard to endure slavery, he said, but look how many do. Who would come to their aid in such a war? Everyone in the world was already under Rome's rule. The only help they could look for would be divine help, and that would be denied them because they would either fight on the Sabbath or be defeated. "All men that go to war, do it either as depending on divine or on human assistance; but since your going to war will cut off both those assistances, those that are for going to war choose evident destruction."

If they did go to war, the Romans would not be generous in victory. Their cities, their temple, their whole nation would be destroyed as an example. Furthermore, all the Jews living throughout the world would die because of this war.

After his speech, Agrippa urged the people to pay the tribute they still owed Caesar and rebuild the cloisters to avoid any appearance of revolution. "For the citadel does not now belong to Florus, nor are you to pay the tribute-money to Florus."

The people of Jerusalem listened to Agrippa and began rebuilding the cloisters. The unpaid tribute of forty talents was collected. But when Agrippa tried to convince the crowds to obey Florus until he was replaced, they cast reproaches on him, had him excluded from the city, even threw rocks at him. Angry at being treated so poorly, Agrippa sent the Jewish leaders to

Florus in Cesarea so he could appoint the country's tax collectors himself, and he returned to his own country.

Rebellion Against Rome

Soon after this, some of the more warlike of the Jews assaulted and took Masada, killing the Romans stationed there and putting their own troops in the fortress. At the same time Eleazar, the temple governor who was the son of Ananias the high priest, persuaded the priests not to accepts gifts or sacrifices from non-Jews. They rejected the sacrifice of Caesar, even though the high priests said that much of the temple itself came from the donations of non-Jews and no one's sacrifice had ever been refused.

Realizing they couldn't stop the impending revolt and knowing they would be the first to be punished for it, the high priests and leaders sent ambassadors to Florus and Agrippa. Simon the son of Ananias led the delegation to Florus; Saul, Antipas, and Costobarus led the one to Agrippa. Both men were asked to bring their armies into Jerusalem and put down the sedition before it became impossible to stop.

Rebellion was exactly what Florus wanted; he sent the ambassadors away without an answer. Agrippa, however, was anxious to save the Jews for the Romans and Jerusalem for the Jews. He sent 3,000 horsemen from Auranitis, Batanea, and Trachonitis to Jerusalem under the leadership of Darius and Philip.

The high priests, Jewish leaders, king's soldiers, and citizens against the revolt seized the upper city. The rebels took the lower city and the temple. War continued between the two groups for seven days, neither willing to give up any of its territory.

The eighth day was the festival of Xylophory, when everyone brings wood to the temple for the perpetual altar fire. Those who held the temple prevented the others from observing the festival. Soon the rebels were joined by many of the sicarii, which gave them the strength to drive the king's soldiers out of the upper city. The house of Ananias the high priest and the castles of Bernice and Agrippa were burned, along with the public archives containing the records of all debts.

Some of the men of power and high priests fled to underground vaults for safety, others to the upper palace with the soldiers. On the following day, the rebels attacked Antonia, besieging the garrison there for two days, after which they took it, killed the soldiers there, and set fire to the garrison. Then they attacked the upper palace, where the battle continued for days.

In the meantime, Manahem the Galilean, the son of Judas, took some men and broke open Herod's armory at Masada, arming his own people and other robbers. He returned to Jerusalem and took over as the rebels' leader. The rebels undermined one of the palace's towers and burned it until it collapsed, only to find its defenders had built a second fortification beyond the tower. At this point the defenders offered to surrender. Manahem accepted the surrender of the king's soldiers and Jewish citizens, but not of the Romans. The remaining Romans fled to the royal towers named Hippicus, Phasaelus, and Mariamne, although Manahem killed many of them before they could reach safety.

On the next day, Ananias the high priest was captured in an aqueduct and killed, along with his brother Hezekiah. Manahem, encouraged by his victories, became so cruel that Eleazar and his men turned against them, attacking them in the temple with the help of many of the people. A few of Manahem's band fled to Masada, but Manahem was captured at Ophla, publicly tortured, and killed.

Metilius, the Roman general, now asked Eleazar's permission to surrender, saying they would give him all they had in return for their lives. Several Jews were sent to pledge the safety of the soldiers, who came out, laid down their arms, and prepared to leave in peace. Once they were disarmed, Eleazar had all of them brutally murdered except Metilius, who promised to become a Jew and was spared. This murder occurred on the Sabbath, which filled the city's citizens with sadness and despair.

Attack on the Syrians

On the same day and hour that the surrendering Roman soldiers were being slaughtered by the Jerusalem rebels, Florus and the people of Cesarea were attacking the Jewish population of that city. They killed over 20,000 in one hour and sent the survivors into slavery; by the end of the day, not one Jew remained.

This total destruction enraged the whole Jewish nation. They divided themselves into several parties and destroyed Syrian villages and the cities of Philadelphia, Sebonitis, Gerasa, Pella, Scythopolis, Gadara, and Hippos. Turning on Gaulonitis, they destroyed and burned cities there, then attacked Kedasa, Ptolemais, Gaba, and Cesarea. Neither Sebaste nor Askelon was able to withstand their attack. When those cities were burned to the ground, they entirely demolished Anthedon and Gaza and the villages around them.

The Syrians killed as many Jews as they lost themselves, until every Syrian city was divided into two opposing camps and the safety of one party lay only in the destruction of the other. The days were spent in fighting, the nights in fear, for if the Syrians destroyed the Jews, they worried about the Jewish sympathizers who remained. Neither side wanted to kill innocent people, so both lived in fear whenever they mingled with the crowds.

Greed increased the bloodshed, since those killed were plundered and those collecting the most booty were the most honored. It was common to see cities filled with the unburied bodies of old men, women, and children.

So far, the conflict had been between Jewish rebels and Syrians, but at Scythopolis, some local Jews fought against their brothers. Indeed, they fought so willingly that the Syrians of Scythopolis suspected them and feared they would turn on them in the night. To prove their loyalty, these Jews were told to take their families out of the city and camp in a nearby grove, which they did for two days. On the third night, the people of Scythopolis attacked, killing 13,000 of them.

Simon

One of the Jews of Scythopolis who fought against the

attacking Jews was a man named Simon, the son of Saul. He was an extremely strong, bold man who fought so well that he was in great measure responsible for the success of the city's defenders. But he was punished for the Jews he killed, for when the people of the city attacked the Jews in the grove, he saw he was doomed and did not attempt to fight back. Instead, he called out that he deserved to die for fighting his brothers and would kill himself so no one could boast of his death. Then he killed his whole family one by one, all of whom seemed to prefer to die at his hands than those of the enemy. Standing on the bodies of his family so everyone could see him, Simon then drove his own sword into his body and died.

Massacres

In addition to Scythopolis, other cities turned against their Jewish citizens. Twenty-five hundred were killed in Askelon. The city of Ptolemais killed two thousand and enslaved many. Tyre killed a great number, imprisoning even more. Hippos, Gadara, and the other Syrian cities killed the boldest of the Jews living there and imprisoned the rest. Only the Antiochians, Sidonians, and Apamians spared the local Jews and refused to imprison them, perhaps because the Jewish population was small in those cities. More than likely, they saw no reason to kill peaceful citizens. The Gerasens also spared their Jews, escorting those who wished to leave safely to their borders.

Agrippa's Kingdom

Agrippa was in Antioch with Cestius Gallus when the revolt began, leaving Noarus in charge of the public affairs of his kingdom. Seventy of the most prominent men of Batanea went to Noarus when the fighting began and asked him for troops to protect their territories. Without Agrippa's consent, Noarus sent his soldiers out in the night to kill the seventy petitioners. When Agrippa heard how cruelly Noarus was treating his kingdom, he immediately took away his procuratorship.

Meanwhile, the rebels took the citadel above Jericho named

Cypros, cut the throats of its defenders, and demolished the fortifications. Another group persuaded the Roman soldiers at Macherus to surrender the fort in exchange for their lives.

Alexandria

The Greeks of Alexandria had been persecuting the Jews there ever since Alexander the Great had given the Jews equal privileges with the Greeks in return for their help against the Egyptians. The Jews of Alexandria lived by themselves in a separate section of the city to avoid being polluted by the Greeks, and although their persecutors were always punished by the governors, they never ceased.

Now that war had broken out in other countries, relations became even more strained in Alexandria, until violence broke out between the Greeks and Jews. Tiberius Alexander, the governor of the city, wasn't able to restore order without the use of force. He sent out two Roman legions and 5,000 additional troops, giving them orders to kill the Jews and plunder their possessions. The soldiers attacked the Delta, which was the Jewish section of town. At first the Jews were able to hold off the troops, but once they were forced to fall back, the Romans killed them unmercifully. In the end, 50,000 Alexandrian Jews were killed before Alexander called off the troops.

Cestius

Cestius, the president of Syria, decided it was time to act. He assembled the twelfth legion from Antioch and 2,000 other troops composed of six cohorts of foot soldiers and four troops of horsemen, plus auxiliaries sent by other area kings. Antiochus contributed 2,000 horsemen, 3,000 footmen, and 3,000 archers. Agrippa sent 3,000 footmen and 1,000 horsemen. Sohemus sent about 1,000 horsemen and 3,000 archers. In addition, the free cities sent troops that were not trained but fiercely hated the Jews. Agrippa accompanied Cestius as a guide and director of what was fit to be done.

Taking some of his forces, Cestius marched to Zabulon, a strong Galilean city called the City of Men that divided the country of Ptolemais from Judea. The citizens of Zabulon had fled to the mountains, leaving their possessions behind; Cestius gave his troops permission to plunder and fire the city. After this, he plundered and burned the whole area before returning to Ptolemais. As soon as Cestius left, the Jews attacked the remaining Syrians in the area, killing about 2,000.

Cestius moved his army to Cesarea, sending part of it ahead to Joppa. He instructed these soldiers to take Joppa by surprise if they could, but wait for him if they were discovered. The force split up and approached Joppa from both the sea side and the land side, taking the unprepared city easily and killing 8,400. Another force was sent to the toparchy of Narbatene, which adjoined Cesarea, to plunder and burn the villages there.

The commander of the twelfth legion, Gallus, was sent to subdue Galilee. Arriving in Sepphoris, his troops were greeted peacefully by the citizens; Sepphoris's example quieted other Galilean cities. The rebels in the area retired to Mount Asamon in the middle of Galilee near Sepphoris, which Gallus attacked. At first, about 200 Romans were lost because the rebels controlled the high ground; the Romans soon outflanked them and killed over 2,000 rebels. Seeing no more signs of revolt in Galilee, Gallus returned to Cesarea.

Jerusalem

Now Cestius began to march on Jerusalem, dispersing some rebels at Antipatris and coming into Lydda. Most of the men of Lydda had left the city to celebrate the feast of tabernacles in Jerusalem. Cestius killed fifty of those left behind, burned the city, and pitched camp at Gabao, about six miles from Jerusalem.

Even though it was the Sabbath, when the rebels of Jerusalem saw Cestius was approaching, they left the feast, took up arms, and fell on the Romans with such strength that their ranks were broken and many of them killed. Cestius's whole army would have been destroyed if his reserves had not turned to support the ranks still standing firm. The Romans lost 515 men; the Jews 22. Among the Jewish dead were Monobazus and Kenedeus, relatives of Monobazus the king of Adiabene.

134

Also lost were Niger of Perea and Silas of Babylon.

When the front of the Jewish army was cut off, they retired to Jerusalem, but Simon the son of Giora attacked the back of the Romans as they climbed up Bethoron, carrying off many of their pack animals and leading them back to town. Cestius stayed on Bethoron for three days, giving the Jews time to take the high parts of Jerusalem, set watches at the city's gates, and occupy the hills outside town around the Roman army.

Seeing that the Roman army was in danger, Agrippa sent Borceus and Phebus, who were both known to the Jews, to encourage the crowd on the hills outside the city to cease fighting. He promised that Cestius would forgive any who joined him. To prevent the crowd from deserting them, the rebels killed Phebus and wounded Borceus. The crowd was outraged at this attack on the ambassadors and beat the rebels with stones and clubs, driving them back into the city.

Cestius saw the disorder of the Jews and attacked with his whole army, driving everyone back into town. He then pitched camp on a hill called Scopus that was a little less than a mile from Jerusalem, but refrained from attacking for three days, hoping some of those inside would surrender. In the meantime, he sent soldiers out to seize wheat from neighboring villages. On the fourth day, he assembled his army and brought it to Jerusalem.

The crowds in Jerusalem were kept in control by the rebels, but the rebels themselves were frightened by the organization of the Romans and retreated to the walled inner city and temple. When he entered Jerusalem, Cestius burned Bezetha (the new city) and the timber market, moved into the upper city, and camped by the royal palace. If he had attempted to take the inner city walls at that point, he could have ended the war that day. But Tyrannius Priscus, the muster-master of the army, and a great many officers of the horsemen had been bribed by Florus; they convinced Cestius to wait.

While Cestius delayed, Ananus, the son of Jonathan, convinced many of the city's leaders that they should open the gates and let Cestius in to put down the revolt. When Cestius was informed of their decision, he refused to believe the offer was serious. The rebels discovered the plot, threw Ananus and his followers off the wall, and drove them into hiding.

The Romans attacked the wall for five days without success. On the sixth day, Cestius attempted to break into the northern quarter of the temple, but the rebels on top of the cloisters beat him off.

The Romans then protected themselves by holding their shields closely together over their heads in tortoise fashion (*testudo*), undermined the wall, and prepared to fire the temple gate. Fearing the city was lost, many of the rebels fled. As they left, the crowds took over the city and made plans to open the gates for Cestius. Had Cestius continued the seige a little longer, he would certainly have taken the city, but he didn't know how close victory was or how much support he had inside the walls. He recalled his soldiers and retreated without cause.

As soon as the rebels saw Cestius's retreat, they regained their courage and attacked the rear of the Roman army. Cestius camped that night at Scopus and retreated further the next day, which encouraged the rebels to punish the rear and flanks of his army all the way. The Romans, thinking a great crowd was chasing them, did not dare turn back and fight those attacking their rear. The rebels attacking the sides of the Roman formation were safe because they were unburdened and fast; the Romans were afraid their ranks would be broken if they paused to fight back. Any Roman who was separated from the army was slain, including Priscus, the commander of the sixth legion, Longinus the tribune, and Emilius Secundus, the commander of a troop of horsemen. With much difficulty, the Romans reached their camp at Gabao.

Cestius stayed at Gabao for two days while the Jews around him grew stronger. On the third day, he decided to escape, ordering most of the pack animals killed and saving only those that carried the army's darts and seige machines. Then he marched toward Bethoron.

The Jews tended to leave the army alone when they were in open places, but when they were forced to descend through narrow passages, the rebels would attack from above and

136

below. Precipices on either side often prevented the Romans from either fleeing or fighting. Their distress was finally so great that they cried out in despair, their cries mingling with the joyful cries of the rebels harassing them. If night had not fallen and saved the army, it would have been destroyed before reaching Bethoron. The rebels took all the places around Bethoron and waited for the Romans to come out of their fortifications.

Cestius knew he could not simply march his army out in the morning and survive. He took 400 of his bravest soldiers, placed them in the strongest fortifications, and told them to raise their flags in the morning as if the whole army were there. During the night, Cestius sneaked the remainder of his army out of camp and moved them four miles away.

When the rebels saw the camp nearly empty in the morning, they killed the 400 soldiers left there and pursued Cestius, but he was too far ahead to be caught. The rebels turned back at Antipatris, captured the discarded Roman equipment, looted the Roman bodies, and returned joyfully to Jerusalem. They had lost only a few men; the Romans lost 5,300 footmen and 380 horsemen.

TEN

After Cestius's retreat, many of the most eminent Jews left the city like rats leaving a sinking ship. Costobarus and his brother Saul left. Philip, the son of Jacimus, who commanded Agrippa's army, left to join Cestius. At their request, Cestius sent Saul and his friends to see Nero in Achia and inform him of the revolt. Cestius blamed Florus for starting the war, hoping thereby to escape punishment himself.

The men of Damascus had already locked the local Jews up and now looked for a way to kill them without their wives, many of whom had become Jews, finding out they were responsible. They fell on the imprisoned Jews and cut the throats of 10,000 of them in one hour.

In Jerusalem, the rebels who returned from chasing off Cestius began to organize themselves. Some of the citizens favoring Rome were overcome by force; others were convinced to join the revolt by the rebels' entreaties. A meeting was held in the temple and generals appointed for the war. Joseph, the son of Gorion, and Ananus the high priest were appointed governors of the city and charged with repairing its walls.

Eleazar, the son of Simon, was not given control of the city because of his tyrannical personality. However, he controlled

139

vast amounts of money he had taken from the Romans in battle, and since that money was badly needed, he obtained a great deal of power despite the wishes of the people.

Generals were chosen for Idumea: Jesus the son of Sapphias, who was one of the high priests, and Eleazar the son of the high priest Ananias. Niger, the governor of Idumea, was ordered to obey these commanders. Other parts of the country received new leaders. Joseph the son of Simon became general of Jericho. Manasseh took over Perea. John the Essen was given the toparchy of Thamma plus Lydda, Joppa, and Emmaus. John the son of Matthias was made governor of the toparchies of Gophritica and Acrabastene. Josephus (the author) the son of Matthias became governor of Galilee and the city of Gamala.

Josephus in Galilee

Josephus's first concern on going to Galilee was to gain the goodwill of the people for the sake of ruling successfully. He knew that by sharing his power with others, he would gain their support, so he chose seventy elders and appointed them to rule Galilee. In every city he chose seven judges to hear minor complaints; major problems involving life and death were to be judged by himself and the seventy elders.

Once the legal system was established, Josephus turned to the protection of Galilee, knowing the Romans would eventually attack it. He built walls around Jotapata, Bersabee, Salamis, Caphareccho, Japha, Sigo, Mount Tabor, Taricheae, and Tiberias. He also walled the caves near Lake Gennessar in lower Galilee as well as places in upper Galilee, the Rock of Achabar, Seph, Jamnith, and Meroth. In Gaulanitis, he fortified Seleucia, Sogane, and Gamala.

The people of Sepphoris were allowed to rebuild their own walls because of their wealth and determination to fight the Romans. John the son of Levi was given permission to build the wall at Gischala for the same reasons.

Josephus then raised a Galilean army of more than 100,000 men, which he armed with old weapons he had collected. He could do nothing about his army's inexperience, but to make them readily obedient, he appointed subalterns after the pattern of the Roman army, dividing his forces into tens, hundreds, and thousands. He taught them basic military maneuvers, conditioned them, and warned them of the skill of the Romans they would fight.

Josephus chose for war 60,000 footmen, 250 horsemen, 4,500 mercenaries, and 600 personal bodyguards. The cities easily maintained the remainder of his army, since each city only sent out half of its men, the rest being left behind to work and farm.

John of Gischala

As Josephus was putting the affairs of Galilee in order, John of Gischala, the son of Levi, was collecting a band of robbers that soon numbered 400. John, a very clever man and a ruthless liar, led his men in robberies throughout Galilee.

John convinced Josephus to let him rebuild the walls of Gischala himself, collecting a good deal of money for that purpose from the town's rich citizens. He also convinced Josephus that the Syrians were anxious to buy oil from Galilee and received a monopoly on the trade, from which he made an enormous profit. At the same time, he encouraged his band of robbers to torment Galilee even more, hoping to either kill Josephus when he came out to put the robbers down or cause the citizens to rise up against him.

At the same time, some young men of Dabaritta robbed Ptolemy, Agrippa's and Bernice's steward, taking from him many expensive clothes, silver cups, and 600 gold pieces. Unable to hide so much wealth themselves, the men brought it to Josephus in Taricheae, who told them he intended to return it to its rightful owners. The men returned home and told everyone Josephus intended to betray them. In the morning, 100,000 men gathered at the hippodrome of Taricheae to threaten Josephus.

All but four of Josephus's friends deserted him. Josephus appeared before the crowd with his clothing torn and ashes on his head in mourning, which led the crowd to believe he was going to confess his betrayal of the robbers. Given permission to speak, he told the people he neither intended to keep the money for himself nor return it to Agrippa; he was merely keeping it safe for use in building the walls of Taricheae. If that was not what they wanted, they could have the money themselves.

The 40,000 in the crowd from Taricheae were delighted; the 60,000 from other cities were not, and a quarrel broke out among them until Josephus promised to use the money to protect all the towns in the area. Most of the crowd dispersed, but 2,000 of them armed themselves and stood outside Josephus's house. Josephus convinced the crowd to send ambassadors inside. Once they were inside, he had them whipped by his guards, then threw them out of the house. On seeing the bloody ambassadors, the crowd dropped its weapons and fled.

Now John of Gischala pretended to be sick and asked permission to go to the hot baths in Tiberias. Josephus suspected nothing and arranged to have the governors of Tiberias house John and provide for him. Within two days, John had convinced the governors to revolt against Josephus. Josephus heard of the plot and marched to Tiberias, where he barely escaped being murdered. After Josephus's escape, John retired to his home in Gischala. Josephus made a public proclamation that in five days he would seize the property of everyone supporting John; 3,000 people surrendered their arms to him.

Now John decided to try diplomacy instead of force, telling the leaders of the revolt in Jerusalem that Josephus was gaining so much power he threatened their leadership. Some of the Jerusalem nobles and rulers secretly sent money to support John against Josephus. In addition, they sent out 2,500 soldiers and several notable men to stir Galilee up against Josephus. Four cities revolted immediately: Sepphoris, Gamala, Gischala, and Tiberias. Josephus took the cities back without a war and sent the notables and their soldiers back to Jerusalem.

Soon Tiberias revolted again, locking its gates against Josephus and urging Agrippa to come take control of the city. Most of Josephus's soldiers were out gathering wheat, so he couldn't use force to reclaim Tiberias. Instead, he collected all the ships on the lake — 230 — and put only four sailors in each boat. He sailed to Tiberias and had the boats sail up and down just far enough from shore that the people in the city couldn't see the boats were empty, then he and seven of his soldiers moved their boat near enough to be seen from the city.

The people of Tiberias, believing all the boats were filled with armed men, surrendered and begged Joseph not to destroy them. He agreed to talk terms with ten of their leaders who joined him on his boat and were then taken out to another ship. Then Josephus asked for fifty city senators as hostages and took them out to a ship. In the end, he captured all 600 members of the city's senate and 2,000 citizens without resorting to arms; all were confined in the prison at Taricheae.

The remaining people in Tiberias called out that a man named Clitus was responsible for the revolt and begged Josephus to punish him and spare the rest of the city. Josephus ordered Levius, one of his seven guards, to leave the boat and cut off both of Clitus's hands; Levius refused to go out into the middle of all the Tiberians alone. Clitus could see how angry Josephus was becoming; he seemed ready to leave the boat and do the job himself, so Clitus begged Josephus to leave him one of his hands, which Josephus agreed to if Clitus would cut off the other hand himself. Clitus drew his sword and cut off his left hand with his right.

A few days later, Josephus retook Gischala, giving his men permission to loot the city, then returning the loot to its owners to obtain their goodwill. He did the same to the cities of Sepphoris and Tiberias.

Once the civil disturbances were put down, the rebels in Jerusalem prepared themselves for war. Ananus the high priest and other powerful men on the rebels' side repaired the walls and saw to the production of arms. Not all the people of Jerusalem supported the revolution; those that didn't were filled with fear. Ananus tried to convince the rebels to restrain the zealots in the city, but failed.

In the Acabbene toparchy, Simon the son of Gioras preferred to torment his citizens instead of rule them; he ravaged the country mercilessly. Finally Ananus and other leaders drove Simon to the fortress of Masada, from which he plundered the country of Idumea until its rulers put soldiers in their towns to protect them.

Nero

Nero was greatly concerned when he heard of the rebellion, blaming Cestius for his own defeat. He believed the best commander for the job of putting down the revolt was Vespasian, an experienced general who had long ago conquered the west for Rome by defeating the Germans and the British. In addition, Vespasian's sons were already Nero's hostages, so there was no doubt of the general's faithfulness.

Vespasian sent his son Titus to Alexandria to bring back the fifth and tenth legions while he traveled by land to Syria to form an army there.

Ascalon

After the rebels had defeated Cestius, they were so confident that they decided to attack Ascalon, an ancient city sixty-five miles from Jerusalem that had always been an enemy of the Jews. The Jewish army was led by Niger the Peraite, Silas of Babylon, and John the Essen. Although Ascalon was strongly walled, the only forces in the area to defend it were one cohort of footmen and one troop of horsemen led by Antonius.

Antonius, not taken by surprise, sent his horsemen out against the larger number of Jews. Although the Jews reached the walls of the city, the horsemen were able to drive them back. The Jews were not a skilled army, but footmen fighting horsemen, poorly armed and undisciplined. They were easily beaten, for as soon as their first ranks fell into disorder, they were chased off by the cavalry into a large plain that suited the horsemen's fighting. By evening, 10,000 Jews had been killed, along with John and Silas; most of the rest were wounded. Niger led the survivors to a small city named Sallis.

Instead of being discouraged by their losses, the Jews decided to try again, even before the wounded had healed. They gathered even more Jews together and attacked the city. This

144

time Antonius laid ambushes for them in narrow passages, killing over 8,000 and forcing the rest to retreat. The Romans pursued the retreating Jews to a fortified tower in a village named Bezedel, fired the tower, and left, assuming Niger would die in the fire. But Niger jumped from the tower and hid in an underground cave for three days, until he heard the Jews searching for his body so they could give him a decent burial. He was greeted joyfully by his men, who believed God had saved him to be their commander during the upcoming war.

Sepphoris

Vespasian reached Antioch (A.D. 67), the third greatest city in the Roman Empire, joined up with Agrippa and his army, and marched to Ptolemais, where he was met by the citizens of Sepphoris, who favored peace with the Romans. Sepphoris had joined with Cestius before Vespasian arrived, promising to fight against their countrymen; now Vespasian gave them horsemen and footmen to protect their city, which was the largest city of Galilee and in a naturally strong location.

Galilee

Phoenicia and Syria encircle upper and lower Galilee. To the west lies the land belonging to the Ptolemais and Mount Carmel, which belongs to the Tyrians. Carmel adjoins Gaba, which is called the City of Horsemen because of Herod's retired horsemen who lived there. To the south is Samaria and Scythopolis, which extend to the river Jordan. On the east are Hippene, Gadaris, Gaulanitis, and Agrippa's kingdom. The north is bounded by Tyre and the country of the Tyrians.

Lower Galilee extends from Tiberias to Zabulon; Ptolemais is its neighbor. Its width extends from the village of Xaloth on the great plain to Bersabe. Upper Galilee's width extends from Baca to Bersabe; its length from Meloth to Thella, a village near the Jordan.

Both Galilees have always been strong, with a large population accustomed to war. The soil is rich and fruitful, cultivated everywhere. Galilee contains a large number of cities and villages full of people; the smallest of them is populated by over 15,000 people.

Perea

Although Galilee seems inferior to Perea because of its size, it is actually stronger, for it is fruitful everywhere. Perea is larger, but a great part of it is desert and rough country. Some parts of Perea produce fruits, and its plains are planted with olive trees, vines, and palm trees. Perea is watered by mountain streams and springs that run even when the streams dry up.

Perea extends from Macherus to Pella; its width from Philadelphia to Jordan. The north is bounded by Pella, the west by Jordan, the south by Moab, and the east by Arabia, Silbonitis, Philadelphene, and Gerasa.

Samaria

Samaria lies between Judea and Galilee. It begins at a village on the great plain named Ginea and ends at the Acrabbene toparchy. In topography, it is the same as Judea, with many hills and valleys that are moist and fruitful. Both have an abundance of fall fruit and derive their water from a generous rainfall; the few rivers they do have are very sweet. Because they have a good supply of grass, their cattle give a large quantity of milk. Both countries are well populated because they are so fertile.

Within Samaria is the village of Anuath (Borceos), which is the northern boundary of Judea. To the south, Judea is bounded by a village named Jordan that is next to Arabia. Its width runs from the river Jordan to Joppa.

Jerusalem is exactly in the country's center, which is why some call it the navel of the country. Judea was divided into eleven portions, of which the royal city of Jerusalem was supreme. Other Judean cities presided over their own toparchies: Gophna, Acrabatta, Thamna, Lydda, Emmaus, Pella, Idumea, Engaddi, Herodium, and Jericho. Jamnia and Joppa presided over their neighboring people.

In addition to these are the Samaritan regions of Gamala, Gaulanitis, Batanea, and Trachonitis, all part of Agrippa's kingdom. The kingdom begins at Mount Libanus and the fountains of Jordan, extending in width to the lake of Tiberias. In length, it runs from the village of Arpha to Julias. Its inhabitants are a mixture of Jews and Syrians.

Josephus Attacks Sepphoris

The Roman army's auxiliaries sent to assist the people of Sepphoris — 1,000 horsemen and 6,000 footmen under the tribune Placidus — pitched camp. The footmen were put within the city to guard it, but the horsemen were camped outside the city walls. These horsemen, by marching continually one way or another and overrunning the adjoining territory, were a problem to Josephus and his forces, since they plundered all the villages not belonging to Sepphoris and intercepted anyone in the open.

Because of this, Josephus marched against Sepphoris, hoping to take the city he had recently fortified. If he could have taken it, the Romans would have been hard put to retake it, but he was unable to take it by force or persuasion.

Josephus's attack provoked the Romans to treat the entire area as a war zone, burning villages, stealing cattle, killing the strong, and enslaving the weak. Galilee was filled with fire and blood, its people's only refuge being the cities recently fortified by Josephus.

Vespasian's Army

Titus returned from Alexandria with the fifth and tenth legions, the most famous legions of all, and joined them to his father's fifteenth legion in Ptolemais. Eighteen cohorts followed these legions. There were also five cohorts from Cesarea with one troop of horsemen and five troops of Syrian horsemen. These ten cohorts each had 1,000 footmen. The other thirteen cohorts each had 600 footmen and 120 horsemen. A considerable number of auxiliaries came from Antiochus, Agrippa, and Sohemus, each of whom contributed 1,000 archers and 1,000 horsemen. Malchus, the king of Arabia, sent 1,000 horsemen and 5,000 footmen, most of whom were archers. The entire army totaled 60,000 besides a vast number of servants who had been trained for war and fought alongside the soldiers they served.

Anyone understanding the Roman army realizes its success resulted from its valor, not from luck. The army was always prepared because of diligent daily exercises. As a result, it never tired in battle, fell into disorder, or yielded to fear; any army less prepared than the Romans was sure to be defeated. It was fair to say the Roman army's exercises were unbloody battles and their battles were bloody exercises.

Sudden strikes and surprises rarely succeeded against the Romans, since they carefully built walled camps as soon as they entered a new area. If the camp's ground was uneven, they leveled it before their large number of carpenters erected its walls and buildings. Each camp was carefully measured and built perfectly square, the troops living within it according to a prearranged design; at no time was the entire army grouped together within its walls.

In addition to the walls, a Roman camp was protected by evenly spaced towers, between which were placed the machines for throwing stones, arrows, and darts. Each of the four walls contained a gate large enough for the camp's animals and for soldiers to make excursions outside the walls. If necessary, a trench six feet deep by six feet wide was dug around the outside of the wall.

Inside the walls, the camp tents were arranged into streets, with the general's tent in the middle. The overall impression was that of a town with a central marketplace, a place for the tradesmen, and an area where officers could meet.

Once secure within its camp, the army lived together by companies, each company having its wood, wheat, and water brought to it when needed and eating as a unit. The whole camp was organized by a system of signals designating times for sleeping, guarding, and rising. In the morning, the soldiers reported to their centurions, the centurions to their tribunes, the tribunes and their officers to the general, who assigned passwords and daily orders.

When camp was to be broken, a trumpet signal notified the soldiers to pack their tents. This was followed by a second signal to load the pack animals, fire the camp, and stand ready to march. A third signal hurried along anyone who might have been a little slow, so no one was out of rank when the army marched. Then the crier stood at the general's right and asked the troops three times, in their native language, if they were ready to go to war. The troops loudly and enthusiastically replied, "We are ready," each time, lifting their right hands as they did so.

On leaving camp, the army marched silently in ranks, as if going to war. Each footman was armed with a breastplate and helmet and carried two swords, one by each side. The sword on the right was no longer than nine inches, while the one on the left was much longer. The footmen guarding the general also carried a lance and buckler in addition to their swords. The rest of the footmen each carried a spear, a long buckler, a saw, basket, pickax, ax, leather thong, hook, and food for three days.

Each horseman carried a long sword on his right and a long pole in his hands. A shield lay alongside his horse, and three or more broad-pointed, spear-length darts in a quiver. He also wore a helmet and breastplate. The troops leading the march were chosen randomly by lot.

Roman Training

The Roman army's fighting was just as organized as its camping and marching. Everything was planned in advance through consultation; as a result, mistakes were seldom made and could easily be corrected. The Romans considered errors made after planning more valuable than unplanned successes, which could lead to thoughtlessness in the future. If they failed, they at least knew they had done their best to avoid it.

Training exercises were designed to strengthen both the bodies and souls of the soldiers. Fear was an important factor in their strength, because capital punishment was the penalty not only for running away but also for the slightest degree of

149

slothfulness and inactivity. Any cruelty arising from this strictness was offset by the rewards bestowed on valiant soldiers.

As a result of this strict obedience, once in battle, the whole army functioned as a single unit. What they did was done quickly, and what they suffered was borne with the greatest patience. With such a well-organized, disciplined, highly trained army, it is no surprise the Roman Empire governed all the inhabitable world of its time.

Vespasian's March

Vespasian marched out of Ptolemais to attack Galilee. First in the line of march were the lightly armed auxiliaries and the archers, who served as scouts. Second were the heavily armed Roman footmen and horsemen. Third were ten men out of every hundred, carrying their arms and the materials needed for setting up camps. These were followed by men whose job was to cut down any woods or smooth any roads hindering the Roman formation in its orderly advance. After these came the commanders' carriages and guards. Vespasian followed with his guards and his legion's cavalry of 120 men. Behind him came the mules carrying the siege machines. The commanders of the cohorts and the tribunes were next in line with their guards, followed by the Roman flags, the eagle, which goes at the head of a legion, and trumpeters.

The main body of the army came next, marching six deep and observed by one centurion marching at its end. Each legion's servants and baggage followed the army. Behind all the legions came the mercenaries, followed by a rear guard of armed footmen and numerous horsemen.

Reaching Galilee, Vespasian pitched camp and waited, to give the rebels time to observe his strength and surrender. Those in Josephus's camp in the city of Garis fled before the Roman army even came in sight; Josephus took those who stayed with him and fled to Tiberias.

ELEVEN

Vespasian marched to Gadara and took it with his first attack because there were so few men of fighting age in the city. Because of his hatred for the Jews and in revenge for Cestius's defeat, he slew all the youth of the city, set fire to it and the villages around it, and carried the remaining inhabitants into slavery.

Josephus retreated to Tiberias, the safest city he could find. His arrival frightened the city's citizens, who decided he must have concluded the war was bound to fail. They were not mistaken; Josephus believed the rebels' only hope of escaping Roman vengeance lay in surrender. Even though he thought the Romans would forgive him, he chose not to dishonor the command he had been given. Instead, he wrote to the leaders in Jerusalem and gave them exact figures on Vespasian's strength, asking for their orders. If they were thinking of coming to terms with Rome, they needed to tell him immediately; if they were determined to fight, he needed more forces.

Vespasian was anxious to destroy Jotapata, having heard that most of the enemy had retreated there and the city was extremely strong. He sent footmen and horsemen ahead to level the road, which was mountainous and rocky, difficult for footmen but impossible for horsemen. His workmen opened a broad path for the army in four days.

On the fifth day (May 21, A.D. 67) Josephus left Tiberias and arrived at Jotapata, raising the spirits of the city. His arrival was reported to Vespasian by a deserter, which made him even more anxious than before to capture the city. He sent Placidus ahead of the army with 1,000 horsemen and the decurion Ebutius, ordering them to encircle the city and prevent Josephus from escaping before the army could arrive.

The following day, Vespasian marched his army to Jotapata, arriving late in the evening. He pitched camp on a small hill just less than a mile from the northern side of the city, making sure his army was visible to the city's defenders, none of whom dared go outside the walls. Vespasian did not attack that evening, because of the long march, but did place a double row of battalions around the city and a third row of cavalry behind them to prevent anyone from getting away. Although this made the Jews despair of escaping, it also made them bolder, for nothing in war makes men fight so desperately as necessity.

When the Romans made an assault the next day, the Jews fought them outside the walls. Vespasian put to work his archers and slingers and all those who could throw from a distance, while he and the footmen ascended a slope from which the city could easily have been taken. Josephus led the Jews out against Vespasian and drove him away from the wall. When the battle ended at the close of the day, the Jews had wounded a great many Romans and killed thirteen. On the Jewish side, seventeen were killed and six hundred wounded.

The following day the Jews, encouraged by their success the day before, again attacked the Romans outside the walls. For five days the fight went on, the Jews unafraid of their enemy's strength and the Romans undiscouraged by the opposition they were meeting.

Jotapata is almost all built on a precipice, having immensely deep and steep valleys on all sides except to the north, where the highest part of the city is built on the mountain's slope. When he had earlier fortified the city, Josephus had built a wall on this slope so no one could seize its top. The city itself is hidden by other mountains all around it and cannot be seen except from nearby.

Vespasian called the commanders under him to a meeting to decide how to assault the city; their decision was to build a bank next to the wall, so Vespasian sent the whole army out to cut down all the trees on the nearby mountains and collect stones. Large panels were set up over the soldiers building the bank, to protect them from the darts being thrown down from the city's wall. Other soldiers tore down the neighboring hills and brought a constant supply of dirt to those building the bank.

One hundred sixty stone- and dart-throwing machines were placed around the city to dislodge the rebels on its wall. Other machines threw lances, seventy-five-pound stones, fire, and arrows. All this, in addition to the archers and soldiers who threw things, made the wall and area next to it too dangerous for the Jews to approach.

Instead, the Jews made sallies outside the wall, pulling away the panels over the Roman workers, killing the exposed Romans, shoveling away the dirt, and burning the bank's wooden parts. To make his workers less vulnerable to this type of attack, Vespasian concentrated them in one area and totally covered them with protective panels. As the bank against the wall grew higher, Josephus put ox hides up to protect his workers and set them to building the wall even higher and adding towers on top. By the time they were done, the wall was thirty feet high.

At this point Vespasian left off direct attacks and decided to starve the city into submission. Jotapata was well supplied with wheat and other necessities, but had no natural source of water except rainwater, and rain was rare at that time of year. To conserve the water they did have, rationing was instituted. The Romans could see the city's people lining up to receive their water rations and took hope from that. Josephus ordered the people to wet their extra clothing and toss it onto the top of the wall until the outside of the wall ran with water. This convinced Vespasian he wouldn't take the city by siege; he went back to his arms, which was what the Jews preferred. If they were going to die, they would rather die in battle than from hunger and thirst.

To obtain needed supplies, Josephus sent people out at night, down a precipitous western valley that was difficult for the Romans to guard. Covering themselves with sheepskins, those sent out were able to smuggle back a large amount of supplies before the Romans caught on and guarded the area more closely.

Josephus believed the city was doomed and started to plan his escape, telling those inside that he could help them more by leaving now and bringing back relief forces than by dying with them. The citizens of Jotapata didn't agree. Seeing he would probably be prevented by force from leaving, Josephus gave up his escape plans and mounted an attack on the Roman camp, destroying tents and burning whatever he found in them. The rebels continued with these sallies day and night for several days.

Soon Vespasian decided to make use of the battering ram, a huge piece of wood armed with a thick piece of iron formed into the shape of a ram's head. The ram was slung in the air by ropes and hung from a strongly supported beam. Pulled back by a large number of men and then thrust forward, the ram was capable of destroying any wall.

First the Romans drove the Jews off the wall, then they moved the ram, which was completely protected by panels and skins on all sides, next to the wall. Its first blow shook the walls. Josephus saw the wall would soon give, so he ordered bags filled with chaff and hung down against the inside of the wall to absorb some of the ram's force and dissipate it. Everytime the Romans moved the ram, the Jews reinforced the wall, until the Romans tied hooks to long poles and cut the ropes holding the bags.

A newly built section of wall began to give way. Josephus and his men made a three-pronged sally outside the wall, setting fire to the machines, protective panels, and banks the Romans had erected. In one hour, everything the Romans had constructed around the wall was destroyed.

Many heroic actions were performed by individual Jews during the battle for Jotapata. Eleazar the son of Sameas, a Galilean from Saab, threw an enormous boulder down onto the battering ram and broke off its head. Jumping down from the wall, he captured the ram's head and carried it back to the top of the wall, ignoring his many wounds. He then jumped down amid the Romans again, taking the ram's head with him.

Next to Eleazar in braveness were Netir and Philip, Galilean brothers from the village of Ruma. They leaped onto the soldiers of the tenth legion with such force and noise that they chased off everyone they attacked. The defenders then burned and buried the machines of the fifth and tenth legions, putting those Romans to flight.

But in the evening, the Romans erected the battering ram again and put it to work against a damaged section of wall. Vespasian was slightly wounded in the foot by a dart, which caused the Romans to pause in the attack until they saw he was not seriously injured. Josephus and his men defended the damaged wall with fire, stones, and iron weapons.

The city was suffering terribly from the Roman bombardment. The force of the stones being thrown in was so great they carried away the pinnacles of the wall and broke the corners off the towers. One stone was capable of injuring several people at once. A man standing near the wall with Josephus was hit so hard by a stone that his head was thrown 2,000 feet from his body. A pregnant woman was hit in the belly; her unborn child landed 300 feet away from her.

The noise of the instruments was terrible, as was the sound of the darts, stones, and bodies being thrown against the walls by their force. The ground inside the walls was covered with blood; so many bodies were piled up against the walls that they could easily have been climbed from the inside. A great many of Jotapata's defenders died or were wounded that night.

The section of wall that had been battered all night finally gave in with the morning, but the Jews were able to raise defenses in the breach before the Romans could enter. After a short rest in the morning, Vespasian tried to draw the defenders away from the broken spot in the wall. Dismounted horsemen covered with armor were placed three deep next to the break, waiting for ladders to be placed so they could storm the hastily built fortification that covered the hole. Behind them Vespasian placed the best of his footmen. The rest of the horsemen were placed all around the wall and into the countryside to prevent escape once the city was taken. The dart throwers and slingers were readied; other troops made ready to erect ladders on the undamaged sections of the wall.

Josephus understood Vespasian's plan. He sent his tired soldiers and the old men to the sound parts of the wall; the strongest men were placed at the breach with six men, one of them Josephus, at their front. He warned those inside to cover their ears and not be frightened by the yell the Romans would soon set up. To avoid the first dart attack, they should fall back a little, fall to their knees, and cover themselves with their armor. Once the Roman archers had emptied their quivers and the ladders were set against the wall, the defenders should go into action. The lamenting women and children were told to be quiet and were locked in their houses.

As Josephus had predicted, the Roman attack began with trumpets and a loud cry followed by the archers' darts. The defenders did as they were instructed while Josephus and his soldiers sallied out to attack the Romans before they could make use of their machinery for scaling the wall. Although they fought bravely, the Jews had no reserves to replace them when they tired, while the Romans kept sending in fresh troops who made good use of their armor and began to scale the wall.

In reply, the Jews poured boiling oil on the Romans coming up the wall, causing them to fall and disperse as the oil ran under their armor and burned its way down their entire bodies. Boiling fenugreek was poured down onto the boards of the Roman scaffolding, causing the soldiers to lose their footing and fall onto the bank, where they were killed by the Jewish archers. At dark, Vespasian called off the attack. That day only six defenders were killed, although over three hundred were wounded. This battle occurred on June 20.

Now Vespasian ordered the banks built even higher and three

fifty-foot towers constructed. These towers, covered with iron plates, were set on the banks so they towered above the city wall. The smaller dart- and arrow-throwing machines were placed on the towers along with the army's best slingers who, protected by the towers' height and fortification, could now safely fire down on the wall's defenders.

Japha

While the fight for Jotapata continued, Vespasian sent Trajan to capture the city of Japha, which had been encouraged to rebellion by the resistance of Jotapata. Trajan, commander of the tenth legion, took 1,000 horsemen and 2,000 footmen to Japha, finding it protected by a double wall.

The defenders of Japha came out to fight Trajan; he soon drove them back behind the first wall, following so closely behind them that the two forces mingled between the walls. When the defenders attempted to flee behind the second wall, those inside the city locked them out to prevent the Romans from entering with them. No amount of pleading would convince the people to open the inner gate.

At this point the Romans shut the first gate and trapped the defenders. Twelve thousand Jews died at Japha that day, cursing not only the Romans but their own people.

Trajan sent for Titus to come and claim the final victory for himself. When the Romans stormed the walls, they found unexpectedly strong resistance waiting for them inside the city; it took six hours for them to subdue the remaining defenders. The women and children of Japha were carried off as slaves and all the men killed. That day, June 25, the total number of Jewish dead from both battles was 15,000; 2,130 were taken captive.

Samaria

Neither did the Samaritans escape their share of misery. They had assembled themselves on Mount Gerizzim, a mountain holy to them, and sallied down to do battle whenever it could be found, until Vespasian decided to stop them. Samaria was well garrisoned with Romans, but the Samaritan rebel army was so large it posed a danger.

Vespasian sent out Cerealis, the commander of the fifth legion, with 600 horsemen and 3,000 footmen. Since the Samaritans held the high ground, Cerealis decided against outright attack. He encircled the mountain and waited the Samaritans out.

The Samaritans were without water on the mountain, and the day was exceedingly hot. While some died of the heat, others fled to the Romans, preferring slavery to death. Hearing how the Samaritans were suffering, Cerealis called up to them to surrender; when they refused, he attacked, killing 11,600. This happened on June 27.

The Fall of Jotapata

By the forty-seventh day of the seige of Jotapata, the Romans' banks were taller than the city's walls. A deserter from the city told Vespasian how desperately tired the city's defenders were and how the last watch of the night always fell asleep at their posts.

Late in the night, the Romans moved quietly to the wall. Titus, the tribune Sabinus, and a few men of the fifteenth legion were the first onto the wall; they quietly cut the throats of the watch and entered the city, followed closely by the tribunes Cerealis and Placidus and their men. By daybreak the citadel was taken and the Romans were in the middle of the city, but most of the citizens were still unaware of the danger: Most were still asleep, and a heavy mist prevented those awake from seeing the Romans clearly.

The Romans drove the people down the precipice from the citadel, the narrow streets and steep grade making it hard for the remaining defenders to keep their footing and fight. Many of those inside killed themselves rather than die at Roman hands.

The Romans might have taken the city without losing a single man if not for Antonius. One of the city's defenders fell into a cavern and offered to surrender to Antonius if he would

158

reach in and help him out. When he reached in, the defender ran him through with his sword.

Everyone who appeared that day was killed by the Romans. On the following days, they searched the underground hiding places and caverns, killing everyone they found except the women and children, whom they took captive. Twelve hundred captives were taken; 40,000 were killed. Vespasian ordered the city demolished and burned. Jotapata fell on July 1.

The Capture of Josephus

After taking the city, the Romans searched for Josephus, believing his capture would shorten the war, but Josephus had jumped into a large pit containing a hidden cave off to its side, where forty other Jews were hiding with enough provisions to last several days. Although he came up at night to search for a way out of the city, the Romans were guarding every possible escape. On the third day, one of the women with them was captured, and their hiding place was revealed.

Vespasian sent the tribunes Paulinus and Gallicanus to give Josephus their promise that he would not be hurt if he surrendered, but Josephus refused until Vespasian sent one of Josephus's old friends, Nicanor, to talk to him. As Nicanor tried to reassure Josephus it was safe to surrender, Josephus recalled several dreams he had had regarding the future of the Jewish and Roman nations. Since he was also a priest, he was well aware of the prophecies of the sacred books. To him, it seemed to be God's will that he live to serve as His minister. Josephus told Nicanor he would surrender.

The other Jews in the cave tried to persuade Josephus not to surrender, reminding him of all the people who had died following him in the fight for liberty. He should kill himself like a man; if necessary, they would kill him. Josephus reminded them it was a sin to kill yourself unnecessarily. Since the Romans had guaranteed his safety, it was God's will he should live. But the others with him were determined they should all die before surrendering, so Josephus tried another approach: If they wanted to die, they should draw lots and kill one

159

another, thus avoiding suicide. Josephus drew one of the two last lots, then convinced the other remaining man to surrender with him after everyone else was dead.

Nicanor led Josephus to Vespasian, who ordered him bound and guarded until he could be sent to Nero. Asking to speak to Vespasian alone, Josephus told him he came as a messenger of God, not as a humble captive. Vespasian was far greater and more powerful than Nero, Josephus told him. He was far more worthy to keep Josephus prisoner, since he would someday rule the empire. Josephus added that he had told the Jewish defenders the exact date the city would fall and that he would be taken captive by the Romans. When Vespasian checked these claims with other captives, they verified them. Both Vespasian and his son Titus decided Josephus might just be a messenger of God, after all; they treated him kindly but kept him a prisoner.

On July 4, Vespasian returned to Ptolemais, then traveled to the seaside city of Cesarea, which was mainly inhabited by Greeks supporting the Romans. The Greeks clamored for Josephus's death. Vespasian ignored them. Two legions were garrisoned in Cesarea for the winter, while the tenth and fifth legions were stationed in Scythopolis.

Joppa

Meanwhile, a great many Jewish rebels had gone to Joppa and repaired it as a place of refuge. The country around the city couldn't support them, so they built a large number of ships and took to piracy around Syria, Phoenicia, and Egypt, making the seas around them unnavigable. When Vespasian attacked Joppa, the rebels fled to safety in their ships.

Joppa was not a natural harbor; the north wind constantly beat on its rocky shoreline and endangered ships near the city. The morning after the rebels left the city in their ships, a "black north wind" fell upon them, dashing many of their ships against the rocks, driving others further out to sea, causing wrecks and drownings. Some of the rebels killed themselves rather than drown; those who were washed on shore alive were killed by the Romans.

The Romans took Joppa unopposed and destroyed it, while 4,200 Jews died at sea in the storm. To prevent any other rebels from using Joppa as a refuge, Vespasian stationed a body of horsemen and a few footmen there with orders to destroy all the villages and cities in the area.

Jerusalem and Tiberias

News of Jotapata's fall soon reached Jerusalem, although at first it wasn't believed because no eyewitnesses were available. As confirmation began to come in, so did rumors of Josephus's death. Jerusalem mourned the death of Jotapata's defenders for the next thirty days. As soon as it was learned that Josephus was alive and being treated far better than the other captives, the citizens of Jerusalem began calling him a coward and a traitor; the fall of Jotapata and their anger at Josephus's survival made the rebels of Jerusalem more determined than ever to fight the Romans.

At Agrippa's invitation to see his kingdom, Vespasian moved his army from Cesarea to Cesarea Philippi for a twenty-day visit and rest. While he was there, news came that Tiberias and Taricheae, two cities in Agrippa's kingdom, had been taken over by the Jewish rebels. Partly as a favor to Agrippa, Vespasian decided to quiet the two cities. He took three legions and pitched camp less than four miles outside Tiberias in Sennabris, then sent the decurion Valerian and fifty horsemen to Tiberias to talk to its citizens, whom he'd heard were loyal to the Romans but being forced to fight by a small number of rebels.

As he approached the city wall, Valerian and his men dismounted to show they had come in peace. At that point, Jesus the son of Shaphat led his band of robbers out against Valerian and his troops. Valerian had no orders to fight and was forced to flee, leaving behind his horses, which Jesus captured.

The leaders of Tiberias were afraid of the Roman response to Jesus' attack. They fled to Vespasian and begged him not to condemn the city because of the few rebels within it. When

Agrippa and Vespasian agreed to their request, Jesus and his men fled to Taricheae; Vespasian entered Tiberias to the welcome of its citizens.

Taricheae

Vespasian now pitched camp between Tiberias and Taricheae, preparing to stay there for some time by heavily fortifying the camp. Because of Taricheae's natural strength, a great number of rebellious Jews had taken refuge there.

Taricheae lay at the base of a mountain on the shore of Lake Gennesareth. Although it was a walled city, its wall was not as strong as Tiberias's, yet the rebels there controlled a large number of armed ships they could flee to if the city were taken.

Jesus and his party attacked the Roman camp before it was secure and destroyed the partially built camp wall, retiring toward Taricheae before the Roman soldiers were able to organize themselves. They were driven by the pursuing Romans to their ships and launched them out just far enough to be able to reach the Romans on shore with their throwing weapons.

Vespasian sent Titus and 600 horsemen to disperse a crowd of citizens gathering on the plain in front of the city. The Romans were greatly outnumbered and sent back for additional forces while Titus encouraged his troops until Trajan arrived with 400 additional horsemen. At the same time, Vespasian sent Antonius and Silo to take the mountain above the city with 2,000 archers and keep the rebels off the city walls. Titus attacked the crowd in front of the city, killing many and forcing the survivors back behind the city wall.

Conflict then broke out within Taricheae between the city's inhabitants and the rebels who were forcing them to fight. When Titus heard the sounds of conflict, he took his forces down to the lakeside and entered the city. The citizens of the city refused to fight for either side and lost many people because of their neutrality; the rebels fought or fled to safety. As soon as the rebels were killed, Titus stopped his men from killing the town's peaceful citizens.

Now Vespasian arrived in Taricheae to set guards and prevent anyone from leaving, preparing ships to chase the rebels out onto the lake.

Jordan and Gennesareth

Lake Gennesareth is named for the country it adjoins. It's five miles wide and seventeen and one-half miles long, filled with pure, sweet water as cool as snow. Several unusual types of fish live in this lake, which is divided in half by the river Jordan.

Panium was once thought to be the headwaters of the Jordan, but Phiala really is. Phiala is fifteen miles from Cesarea, close to the road on the right as you travel toward Trachonitis. Its water fills the pool to the top, never sinking or running over. This pool was discovered while Philip was tetrarch of Trachonitis when he had chaff thrown into the water at Phiala that later surfaced at Panium.

Jordan's visible stream arises in the cavern at Panium, then divides the marshes and fens of Lake Semechonitis. After another fifteen miles, the river passes Julias, goes through the middle of Lake Gennesareth, then over a desert to its exit in Lake Asphaltitis. The country around Lake Gennesareth is beautiful and fruitful, supporting walnut trees, palms, figs, and olives, all of which require various climatic conditions for growth. Grapes and figs grow there continually for ten months of the year, and other fruits are available year round. In addition to its favorable air temperature, Gennesareth is liberally watered by a mountain named Capharnaum. Gennesareth stretches along the lake's banks for three and three-quarter miles; its width is two and one-half miles.

The Battle of Lake Gennesareth

Once Vespasian's ships were ready, he put the needed troops on board and set sail after the Jews on the lake. These rebels couldn't land on the occupied shore, but neither could they defeat the Romans, who outnumbered them on the lake. When they came close enough, they would throw stones at the

Romans, only to have them bounce off the Romans' armor; those who attempted to fight were killed by the Romans' long poles. Sometimes the Romans boarded the rebels' ships and killed them in hand-to-hand fighting. If they tried to escape to the shore, the Jews were caught between the land troops and those leaving their boats to chase them. In the end, the lake's water was blood red and all the rebels from the boats lay dead.

The days that followed were filled with the stench of the unburied bodies that washed up along the shoreline. The total number killed on the lake and land was 6,500.

When the battle was over, Vespasian held a tribunal to decide what to do with the citizens of Taricheae, since it was outsiders who had begun the battle, not the city's residents, and the people themselves had refrained from fighting.

His commanders believed that setting these people free would not be to the Romans' advantage, since they would have no homes and would only encourage those to whom they fled to fight the Romans. Vespasian was reluctant to order the death of the inhabitants of the city himself, especially since he had given his word they wouldn't be harmed. He gave his commanders tacit permission to do as they wanted and permitted the Jews to leave the city only by the road to Tiberias. Once in Tiberias, they were locked inside the gates and assembled in the stadium. The old men and other useless people were killed — 1,200 of them. Six thousand of the strongest young men were sent to Nero as slaves, to dig a canal for him. Agrippa was given permission to dispose of all the people from his kingdom and sold them into slavery. The rest — 30,400 — were sold into slavery. This battle occurred on September 8.

TWELVE

After the taking of Jotapata and Taricheae, most of the rebellious Jews in Galilee surrendered to the Romans, with only those on Mount Tabor and the cities of Gischala and Gamala holding out. Gamala was a city across the lake from Taricheae, bordering on Agrippa's kingdom with Sogana and Seleucia.

Gamala, Sogana, and Seleucia were parts of Gaulanitis. Sogana was in Upper Gaulanitis, Gamala in Lower Gaulanitis. Seleucia was by Lake Semechonitis, a lake eight miles wide and sixteen miles long. Its marshes reached as far as Daphne (possibly Dan) and contained springs that supplied water to what was called Little Jordan, under the temple of the golden calf, where it joins the Great Jordan.

Agrippa had made treaties with Sogana and Seleucia at the beginning of the revolt, but Gamala had refused, relying on its natural defenses, which were greater than Jotapata's. Gamala was situated on a rough ridge of a high mountain, on a site resembling a camel's hump, from which it got its name. The sides and face of this ridge ended in vast, deep valleys. Only the back, where the city joined the mountain, was approachable, and the city's residents had cut a ditch there to protect that approach.

The houses of Gamala were built very close to one another on the city's steep slope; its immensely tall southern mount served as the city's citadel. Above the citadel was an unwalled precipice extending to a great depth. At the edge of the city within the wall was a spring of water.

Josephus had walled the city, adding ditches and underground mines. There were fewer fighting men in Gamala than there had been in Jotapata, but they were confident of their city's strength, since Agrippa had previously besieged it for seven months without success.

Vespasian came to Gamala from Emmaus, where he had camped before Tiberias. Because of its situation, he couldn't encircle the city, but he placed men wherever possible and took the mountain overlooking the city. While his soldiers on the mountain built their own fortifications, Vespasian began building banks at the bottom, on the eastern side of the city where the highest tower was situated and the fifteenth legion was camped. The fifth legion took its position against the center of the city, while the tenth legion filled up the ditches and valleys.

King Agrippa approached the city wall to encourage the people inside to surrender, only to be hit on the right elbow by a stone. This angered the Roman soldiers, who saw the inhabitants as cruel men who would attack a fellow Jew trying to help them out of their difficulties.

The Roman banks were finished rapidly and the seige machines brought up. Chares and Joseph, the city's leaders, readied their men for war and sent them up onto the wall. For a while they hindered the placement of the machines but were soon driven back by the stones and darts thrown from the machines already in position. The Romans brought their battering rams to three locations, broke the wall, and attacked the people inside the city.

Once inside, the Romans found themselves overpowered by the city's defenders and driven into the upper parts of the city. There they were attacked by the people in that section and driven back down the steep streets into the city's houses. The houses were unable to support the weight of the heavily armored soldiers and began to collapse, the ones above taking down those below and killing many of the Romans inside. The people of the city saw this collapse as God's assistance and pressed forward, using the stones from the rubble and captured Roman swords as their weapons.

Those soldiers able to find their way out of the dust-choked city retreated, but Vespasian stayed, working his way back toward the higher parts of the city until he suddenly found himself nearly alone. He and his men covered themselves with their shields in a *testudo* formation until his attackers retired and he could retreat outside the city's wall.

A great number of Romans died in this battle, including the decurion Ebutius, who had done great damage to the Jews in other battles. A centurion named Gallus and ten of his soldiers hid themselves inside a house where they overheard the house's Syrian inhabitants planning what to do about the Romans. In the night, Gallus cut the throats of those in the house and escaped with his men.

Vespasian encouraged his men in camp, and the people of Gamala rejoiced over their victory while worrying about the battle still to come. When the Romans raised their banks and attempted to enter the city again, a large number of people from the city fled through the deep unguarded valleys and the underground caverns. Those who stayed inside began to die from starvation, since the city's food had been collected for use by the fighting men.

While this seige continued, Vespasian decided to subdue the rebels who had seized Mount Tabor, which was situated between the great plain and Scythopolis. Mount Tabor is three and three-quarter miles high, incapable of being climbed on its north side. Its top is a plain of three and one-quarter miles surrounded by a wall (the actual figures may be more like one-half mile tall with a plain of three-quarters of a mile on top). Josephus had walled Mount Tabor in forty days and stocked it with food and water. Since a great number of people had gathered there, Vespasian sent Placidus and 600 horsemen to take the mountain.

Placidus knew he couldn't climb the mountain and take it by force, so he called up and asked the people to come down and surrender. They came down intending to attack Placidus, not surrender. When he saw their intentions, Placidus pretended to run from the crowd, led them out onto the plain, then swung around and encircled the crowd. The surviving rebels fled to Jerusalem, while those living in the area came to terms with Placidus.

The fighting men inside Gamala resisted the seige until October 22, when three soldiers of the fifteenth legion got under a tower and undermined it. The noise of the falling tower caused many of the city's defenders to try to escape, including their leader Joseph, who was killed as he tried to leave through the broken wall. Chares, the city's other leader, died of natural causes aggravated by fear.

Remembering their first failure, the Romans held off entering the city until October 23. Then Titus took 200 horsemen and some footmen and entered the city noiselessly. Some of the citizens fled to the citadel, while others met Titus in battle and were killed.

Vespasian attacked the citadel, which had the advantage over him until a great wind came up that favored the Romans attacking from below. Four thousand people on the citadel were killed by the Romans; 5,000 threw themselves to their death. Only two people escaped from the citadel alive: the granddaughters of Jacimus, a former general of Agrippa's army. Gamala first revolted on September 24; it fell on October 23.

Gischala

The only remaining Galilean city to be taken was Gischala. Its inhabitants, most of them farmers, were anxious to make peace with the Romans, but some of the city leaders and all of the robbers taking refuge there preferred to fight under the leadership of John the son of Levi.

Vespasian sent Titus and 1,000 horsemen toward Gischala, withdrawing the tenth legion to Scythopolis and accompanying the other two legions to Cesarea for a period of rest. Jerusalem still remained to be taken, a difficult task because of the number of rebels gathered there and its strong defenses. To prepare his men for that battle, Vespasian rested and exercised them.

Titus saw it would be easy to take Gischala on the first attempt but knew if he did, the crowds within would be killed by his soldiers. He was tired of blood and pitied the innocent who would die with the guilty, so he called up to those on the wall and asked them to surrender the city in exchange for their safety. None of the city's residents dared reply or even climb to the top of the wall; John's forces were preventing anyone from leaving the city, surrendering, or opening the gates to the Romans.

John replied to Titus that he was personally willing to come to terms but could not force the others to do the same. However, he said he could make neither peace nor war on the Sabbath. Would Titus be willing to wait until that was over before they discussed terms? He could easily surround the city to prevent them from fleeing while he waited, if he wanted to.

In truth, John had less regard for the Sabbath than for his own survival and planned to escape the city during the night. And this preservation of John was the work of God, who used him to bring on the destruction of Jerusalem. It was also His work that Titus accepted John's proposal and withdrew his horsemen to Cydessa.

In the night, once John saw there was no Roman guard around Gischala, he and his men fled toward Jerusalem with many of the city's people. In addition, he took a great number of women and children two and one-half miles from the city before abandoning them. The women and children begged John to wait for them; many lost their way in the dark or were killed in the panic that followed, while the rest fled or hid the best they could.

When Titus came to the wall to arrange terms the next day, the remaining citizens of Gischala opened the gates to him, told him of John's flight, and begged for his mercy. Titus sent part of his troops after John, but he was already safely inside Jerusalem. Six thousand of the fleeing women and children were killed by the Romans; 3,000 were taken captive and returned to Gischala.

Titus entered the city to the acclaim of the crowds, ordering his men to pull down a small section of the city's wall as a sign the city had been taken in war. He refrained from killing the crowds or trying to separate the guilty from the innocent, being content with threats and leaving a garrison behind to keep the peace and put down any further revolts.

All Galilee was now taken, but at a great cost to the Romans.

When John and his men entered Jerusalem, thousands of people crowded around to ask what had happened. Still breathing heavily and sweating from his flight, John assured them everything was under control. He had simply decided it would be best to fight the Romans at Jerusalem. No mention was made of his hasty flight from the Romans, but some of the crowd realized John's "retreat" was no more than outright flight.

John was totally unconcerned about those he had left behind. The Romans were weak, he said, while he was strong, and the walls of Jerusalem were perfectly capable of withstanding any Roman attack. John's harangues encouraged a great number of the city's young men, making them anxious for war against the Romans, but those older and wiser knew what was coming and lamented.

The Zealots

Even before the rebellion of Jerusalem, the whole country had fallen into disorder. Titus went back from Gischala to Cesarea. Vespasian took Jamnia and Azotus, putting garrisons in them and bringing a great number of people back with him who had gone over to the Roman side.

Seditions broke out in every area, those who supported the Romans fighting those who didn't, with the rebels pillaging and robbing the people of the country more severely than the Romans ever did. The Roman garrisons guarding the cities did little to protect them from the robbers, partly because of their hatred for the Jews and partly to avoid unnecessary combat.

Eventually the leaders of these bands of robbers were satisfied. They gathered together from all over the country and went to Jerusalem in a body. Jerusalem at this time had no governor and had always welcomed Jews from outside. The people of Jerusalem believed the robbers had come to help defend their city and made them welcome. In reality, they were a useless and expensive burden on the city, eating up its provisions before the battle for the city ever began.

Other robbers joined the plundering within Jerusalem, but these more wicked ones turned to open murder of some of the city's most eminent citizens. The first man they meddled with was Antipas, a man from the royal family who controlled the public treasures. They locked him up, along with Levias and Sophas, who were also from the royal family. In addition to these three, they captured the other principal men of the country, causing everyone in the city to protect themselves as though they were living in a state of war.

The robbers knew public sentiment would prevent their keeping these powerful men prisoner for long and attempts would be made to free them, so they decided to have them killed. They sent John the son of Tabitha, the most bloody-minded of them all, with ten others to cut the throats of all their prisoners, then told the people these leaders had been secretly meeting with the Romans to arrange the city's surrender.

The High Priesthood

By now the people of Jerusalem were in such a state of fear that they allowed the robbers to get away with appointing the high priests themselves. These men annulled the ancient line of succession and ordained unknown common men to that office. They also set the city's leaders at odds with one another by various tricks and thereby took control of the city. Satisfied with their unjust actions toward men, they then turned their contempt to God and entered the sanctuary with unclean feet.

The zealots, as they now called themselves, turned the temple sanctuary into their own personal refuge, demonstrating their power by sending for one of the priestly tribes, the tribe of

171

Eniachim, and casting lots to decide who of that tribe should be appointed high priest. The lot fell to Phannias the son of Samuel, from the village of Aphtha, a man not only unworthy of the office but so ignorant he didn't even know what the high priesthood was. They brought the unwilling man into the city, adorned him with the sacred garments, and told him precisely what to do on every occasion.

Civil War

The people of Jerusalem rebelled at this sacrilege, encouraged by Gorian the son of Josephus and Symeon the son of Gamaliel. The most respected of the high priests, Jesus the son of Gamala and Ananus the son of Ananus, reproached the assembled crowds for their laziness and excited their anger at the zealots, urging them to overcome them by force before the city and temple were totally destroyed. The crowd, now more than willing to rid themselves of the zealots, chose Ananus their leader.

While Ananus was picking out his army and readying them for the fight, the zealots heard of his plan, dashed out of the temple in raiding parties, and spared no one they encountered. The populace assembled by Ananus was poorly armed and untrained, but they outnumbered the zealots and were every bit as committed as the zealots themselves.

At first the two groups only attacked at long range, with stones and javelins, but whichever group was the strongest in any individual encounter soon used their swords, and a great number died on both sides. The people carried their wounded and dead back to their houses, but the wounded zealots all retreated to the temple, polluting its sacred floor with their blood.

In these conflicts, the zealots always sallied out of and returned to the temple, which angered the people so much that they eventually beat them all back into the temple. Ananus and his men charged into the Court of the Gentiles after the zealots, who fled to the inner court and shut its gates.

Ananus thought it improper to attack the holy gates or open

them to the unpurified crowds; he chose 6,000 men to guard the cloisters on a rotating basis and keep the zealots confined.

John of Gischala had kept his distance from the zealots while directing them. Now he pretended to side with Ananus, following him around every day and secretly reporting all he heard being planned to the zealots inside the temple. In a few days, Ananus began to suspect John was the zealots' source of information. He was required to take an oath of loyalty to the people, but once the oath was given, their suspicions were eased so much that they made John their ambassador to the zealots, hoping that bargaining would avoid further pollution of the temple.

John entered the temple and told the zealots an outright lie, saying Ananus was sending ambassadors to Vespasian to urge him to come and take the city. If they were wise, he said, the zealots would choose one of two courses: They should either convince the guards to help them escape or they should send for help from outside the city. There was no hope that the citizens of Jerusalem would forgive them.

The Idumeans

Even though John's speech was designed to alarm the zealots, he didn't quite dare name the outside help he referred to, although he hinted that it was the Idumeans. To stir up the leaders of the group even more, he told them of a cruel plot Ananus was planning against them personally — a plot John had just invented, as he had lied when he said Ananus had sent for Vespasian. Eleazar the son of Simon, the most intelligent and capable of the zealots, and Zacharias the son of Phalek, both of whom came from priestly families, considered what they should do. They feared there was no time to send for help before Ananus or Vespasian attacked. Nevertheless, they wrote a letter to the Idumeans claiming that Ananus was forcing the people to turn the city over to the Romans. They had revolted from the rest, they said, but needed help immediately to save the city.

Two men named Ananias were chosen to deliver the letter to the Idumeans; besides being excellent speakers, they were both fast runners. There was no doubt the Idumeans would respond swiftly to this request, being a very excitable and disorderly people who only needed a little flattery and petitioning to make them eager for a fight. The rulers of Idumea were dismayed by the letter and the additional information provided by the runners. They called their people together for war and assembled an army of 20,000 in a very short time, then marched to defend their holy city. The four Idumean commanders were John; Jacob the son of Sosas; Simon the son of Cathlas; Phineas the son of Clusothus.

No one in the city had seen the two messengers leave, but the approaching Idumeans were spotted in time for the city gates to be closed and guarded against them. Jesus, the eldest high priest except for Ananus, stood on the tower above the Idumeans to tell them there was no truth in the zealots' claims that they were going to turn the city over to the Romans. The zealots were no more than impious robbers, he said. If the Idumeans wanted to enter the city unarmed, they could see for themselves the damage done by the zealots and how they had polluted the temple. They could even serve as judges between the city's citizens and the zealots, if they wished. Or they could join in putting the zealots down. If none of those paths of action seemed right to them, Jesus asked the Idumeans to leave the city alone until they could prove the zealots' charges and stop complaining that the gates were shut against them.

The Idumeans were so furious at being locked out of the traditionally open city that they totally ignored Jesus's words. Simon, one of their leaders, replied that it was no wonder those who loved liberty were locked in the temple, when the priests dared to lock the gates of the common city against their own people. The Idumeans would stay in front of the walls in their armor until either those inside repented of their actions or the Romans tired of waiting to be admitted.

Jesus left the wall sadly. Now the city was besieged from inside and out. As for the Idumeans, they were beginning to wish they'd stayed home. Where was the strength the zealots had bragged of? Still, leaving without accomplishing anything would cause them shame. They camped outside the wall for the night, enduring a great storm that seemed to portend future calamities.

Breakout

As the storm continued, Ananus gave the guards in the cloisters overlooking the temple permission to sleep. While they did, some of the zealots used the saws in the temple to cut the bars of one temple gate, the noise of the sawing being covered by the fury of the storm. Once out of the temple, the escaped zealots opened the city gate by the Idumeans and let them in. If they had attacked the city that night, it would easily have been taken; instead, the zealots convinced them to go to the temple and free the zealots still captive before the guards were warned and woke the city.

Together, the zealots and Idumeans overpowered the sleeping guards in the cloisters, whose screams woke the city. Armed men ran to the temple to prevent the zealots from escaping. As long as they thought they were only fighting the zealots, they fought bravely, but once they recognized the Idumeans, many of them threw down their arms and began to lament.

The Idumeans spared no citizens at the temple, being naturally a barbarous and bloody people, killing both those who fought and those who begged to be spared. By daybreak, eighty-five hundred bodies lay in the outer temple, which was totally awash in blood. Now the Idumeans attacked the city itself, plundering every house and killing anyone they met before searching for and slaughtering the high priests, then casting their bodies away without burial.

The death of Ananus was the beginning of the destruction of Jerusalem, and from that day the overthrow of the wall and the ruin of the city's affairs may be dated. Ananus was on all accounts a just and venerable man, a lover of equality and liberty who thought of the public's welfare before his own and preferred peace above all else. He knew the Romans were unconquerable and the Jews would be destroyed unless they made peace with them. If Ananus had lived, he would have saved Jerusalem.

Although Jesus, who also died that day, was not as great as Ananus, he was far superior to others. It could only be because God had doomed Jerusalem to destruction that He allowed these defenders to be killed and cast out naked to be eaten by the dogs and wild animals.

The Slaughter

After the high priests were dead, the Idumeans fell on the city's common citizens and killed them wherever they were found. The noblemen and youth were imprisoned in hopes they would join with the zealots. When not one of them would, they were scourged and tortured, then finally put out of their misery. Those they captured during the day were killed during the night and their bodies thrown away to make room in the prison for more.

No one left alive dared to weep openly for their slain relatives or bury them, for anyone caught mourning soon joined those they mourned. Only in the night could they safely take up a little dust and scatter it on the bodies, even though some were bold enough to do so in the daytime. Twelve thousand of the city's better people died in this massacre.

The zealots and Idumeans soon became bored with simply killing men; they began setting up illegal tribunals and judges. Seventy of the city's most prominent men were assembled as if they were real judges, and Zacharias the son of Baruch was brought before them. This Zacharias was a lover of freedom and justice, a wealthy and influential man who could do the zealots great harm. He was accused of sending to Vespasian and betraying the city, although there was no proof of this; the zealots' words were the only proof required.

Zacharias saw he was doomed and had nothing to lose; he stood up, laughed at the accusation, and quickly denied the charges. After that, he turned on the zealots and enumerated their transgressions of the law, lamenting the current state of public affairs. Although they were furious, the zealots controlled themselves to give the appearance of a legal trial. They were also interested in seeing whether the judges were more committed to justice than to their own lives.

The seventy judges found Zacharias innocent, choosing to die with him before being responsible for his death. Two of the boldest of the zealots fell on Zacharias, killed him in the middle of the temple, mocked him, then threw his body into the valley below the temple. Although the zealots struck the judges with the backs of their swords, they were freed to spread the message that there was no justice in Jerusalem and its citizens were no better than slaves.

The Idumeans Leave Jerusalem

The Idumeans were becoming displeased by what was happening to Jerusalem; the zealots were becoming anxious to have the Idumeans gone. One of the zealots came to them privately and encouraged the Idumeans to return to their homes before they were blamed for the destruction of Jerusalem. The Romans were not yet expected, the walls were strong, and it was time to cut their ties with the zealots and escape further blame for their actions.

The Idumeans thought this was good advice. To everyone's surprise, they freed 2,000 people being held in prison and left the city. The people were encouraged to see so many of their enemies had left; the zealots were equally happy to be relieved of those who could have hampered them in their plans.

Now the zealots began to kill anyone in the city they envied or feared. Gorion, a prominent and outspoken man, was eliminated. Niger of Perea, a valiant general of the Jewish forces, was dragged out of the city to be killed. When he asked to be properly buried, his request was denied. As the zealots attacked him, Niger cursed them, praying they might undergo both famine and pestilence in the war, as well as turn to slaughtering one another.

No one was safe from the zealots, no matter how they acted. Those who disagreed with them were killed. Those who didn't were watched until an excuse was found for their death. Those who stayed away from them were condemned as proud men; those who approached boldly were coming to condemn them. Those offering help were suspected of plotting. The poor and rich suffered together, and the only punishment for any offense was death.

The Roman commanders, hearing of the civil war in Jerusalem, encouraged Vespasian to attack the city while it was divided, but Vespasian thought it better to let the Jews eliminate one another for a while; an attack now would only unite them.

As time passed, more and more Jews escaped from Jerusalem, although all the exits were guarded by the zealots. Still, those who knew who to bribe were allowed to leave, with the result that the rich were able to escape but the poor remained behind to be killed.

Dead bodies were left to putrify in the sun by the sides of the roads and within the city, in defiance of the law. The prophets were laughed at, although they foretold that Jerusalem would be taken in war and destroyed once sedition took over the Jews and they polluted their temple.

John of Gischala

By now, John was beginning to think of himself as the only man fit to lead the zealots. He joined the most wicked group of them all and broke off from the others. Some of the zealots submitted to John's tyrannical leadership out of fear; others he charmed into joining him, while still more began to think it safer to have one man take the blame for everyone's actions.

The main reason some opposed John was their dread of monarchy, knowing he would never give up total power once he obtained it. So the rebels divided into two parties. They refrained from fighting with each other but competed to see which group could capture the biggest prey.

The people of Jerusalem were now beset by war, tyranny, and sedition. Many of them decided war was the least of the three evils and fled to foreign countries, where the Romans would give them the protection they couldn't find among their own people.

THIRTEEN

Not far from Jerusalem was the ancient fortress of Masada, now controlled by the sicarii. These men had previously overrun the neighboring countries, but were now only going out to obtain what was needed for survival. Hearing that the Romans were resting in camp and the Jews were divided among themselves in Jerusalem, the sicarii became bolder. During Passover, they came down by night and overran the small city of Engaddi, throwing its citizens out and killing over 700 women and children. After plundering the town and taking all the fruits that flourished there, they returned to Masada. Further expeditions followed as the sicarii ranks were swollen by other corrupt men arriving at Masada, until the whole countryside of Judea, which had been peaceful, was now in danger and disorder.

Vespasian

Vespasian heard of the unrest in the countryside and within Jerusalem, but before he could attack the city, he needed to put down the problems in the countryside. Therefore he marched against Gadara, the main city of Perea, entering it on March 4, 68 at the invitation of the city's leaders who had asked him to put down the rebels there. The rebels prepared to flee the Romans, but decided it would be dishonorable to run without first shedding a little blood. They captured Dolesus, a prominent man who probably had called in the Romans, killed him, and treated his body in a barbarous manner before fleeing.

The people of Gadara admitted Vespasian with joy, accepting his pledge of security, and welcomed the garrison he left behind for their defense. They even tore down the city's wall before Vespasian asked them to, as a sign of their loyalty.

Vespasian returned to Cesarea with most of his troops, leaving Placidus behind with 500 horsemen and 3,000 footmen to deal with the rebels who had fled the city. When they saw the Romans, the rebels had gone to the village of Bethennabris and armed the many young men there, some by force. Now they rashly assaulted Placidus. The horsemen at first gave way to entice the rebels away from the village's wall, then encircled and held them while the footmen attacked.

Those who escaped the Roman trap fled toward the village wall, but the guards on the wall didn't know what to do. They wanted to admit their own people, but not the Romans who were so close behind them. They barely managed to save their own people while keeping out the Romans. By dark, Placidus had taken the village and plundered it, while those who managed to escape into the countryside made it seem as if the whole Roman army had attacked them, which convinced many of the neighboring people to flee toward Jericho with them.

Placidus sent his horsemen after them, driving them toward the rain-swollen Jordan River, where they were forced to fight. In the hand-to-hand combat that followed, 15,000 Jews were killed. A great number perished when they were forced into the river, and twenty-two hundred were taken prisoner, along with many asses, sheep, camels, and oxen. This destruction, while it was great, appeared worse than it was because of the large number of bodies filling the Jordan and floating down the river into Lake Asphaltitis.

Placidus now fell on the neighboring cities and villages, taking Abila, Julias, Bezemoth, and everything as far as Lake Asphaltitis. He then put his soldiers on ships and killed those fleeing onto the lake. By the time he was done, all of Perea as far as Macherus had either surrendered or been taken by the Romans.

The March to Jericho

In the meantime, Vespasian received word that Vindex and the other Galatian leaders had revolted from Nero. Foreseeing civil war disrupting the empire, Vespasian decided to win the war with the Jews as rapidly as possible and secure the eastern part of the empire for Rome.

Winter prevented him from going into the field, but while he waited for spring, Vespasian put garrisons in the villages and small cities and rebuilt many of the destroyed cities. When spring came, he took the greatest part of his army from Cesarea to Antipatris, spending two days there to settle the city's affairs. On the third day he marched on, destroying the neighboring villages and everything in the toparchy of Thammas. He moved on to take Lydda and Jamnia, then settled many of the Jews who had come over to his side there. Reaching Emmaus, Vespasian took all the roads leading to Jerusalem, fortified his camp, and left the fifth legion there.

Arriving in the toparchy of Bethletephon, he burned the city and its villages, then fortified the strongholds in Idumea. In two Idumean villages — Betaris and Caphartobas — he killed over 10,000 and captured over 1,000. The rest of the villages' citizens were driven out so a large number of Roman soldiers could use the villages as bases for destroying the whole mountainous area.

The Region of Jericho

Vespasian returned to his camp in Emmaus before attacking Samaria. On June 2, he pitched camp near the city of Neapolis (or Sichem or Mabortha). On the second day, he went to Jericho, where Trajan joined him with his army.

A great crowd came out of Jericho at Vespasian's approach and fled to the mountains next to Jerusalem; those left behind were largely killed, and the city was desolate.

Jericho was situated on a plain overlooked by a barren mountain range stretching from Scythopolis and Sodom on the north to Lake Asphaltitis on the south. On the other side of the Jordan was another mountain range running from Julias on the north to Somorrhon (possibly Gomorrah), at the boundary of Petra, on the south. This ridge contained the mountain called the Iron Mountain, which ran as far as Moab.

The region between these ridges was called the great plain, an area twenty-eight and three-quarter miles long and fifteen miles wide, divided in the middle by the Jordan. The plain stretched from the village of Ginnabris to Lake Asphaltitis and contained two lakes: Asphaltitis and Tiberias. Asphaltitis was a salt lake; Tiberias sweet and fruitful. In the summer, the plain was a desert, except around the Jordan River, where palms grew.

Despite the area's dryness, there was a plentiful fountain rising near the old city of Jericho that Joshua the son of Nun took from the Canaanites. Originally this fountain was unhealthy, but it was gentled and made healthful by the prophet Elisha, the disciple of Elijah, who threw salt into the fountain and prayed it might become fruitful. He also prayed that the air would become more temperate and give the people many fruits of the earth and many children. He asked that the spring never fail as long as the people continued to be righteous. Ever since then, the spring proved faithful and extremely good for watering crops.

This spring watered a larger area of land than any other waters do, passing through a plain eight and three-quarter miles long and two and one-half miles wide, nourishing gardens thick with trees. The area produced honey, balsam, cypress, and trees producing myrobalanum.

If the water there was drawn before dawn and exposed to the air, it became exceedingly cold in contrast to the summer air. In the winter, it became warm. The air of the country was so warm that people dressed in linen even when snow covered the rest of Judea. This area was eighteen and three-quarter miles from Jerusalem and seven and one-half miles from Sordan. Between Jericho and Jerusalem the land was a stony desert, as was the land to Jordan and Lake Asphaltitis.

Lake Asphaltitis

Lake Asphaltitis was bitter and unfruitful, so salty that everything floated on it. When Vespasian went to see it, he ordered some men who could not swim bound and thrown in; they floated easily. The lake changed color three times a day as the sun's rays changed, and it threw up black clots of bitumen in many places, which floated on the water like headless bulls. The people of the area collected these clots in their boats, which would become mired by the clots until dissolved free with menstrual blood or urine. The bitumen was used in many medicines and for caulking ships. Lake Asphaltitis was seventy-two and one-half miles long, extending as far as Zoar in Arabia. Its width was eighteen and three-quarter miles. The country of Sodom bordered the lake.

Sodom had been a happy, fruitful area before it was burned by lightning because of the impiety of its inhabitants. Remainders of that fire were still visible, and the traces (or shadows) of the five cities there were still to be seen. Although the fruits that grew there looked fit to eat, they dissolved into smoke and ashes on being picked.

Nero's Death

Vespasian had now fortified all the places around Jerusalem and built citadels at Jericho and Adida. Lucius Annius had been sent to take Gerasa and the area around it. Once that was done, all the territory around Jerusalem was in the control of the Romans, leaving the people of the city trapped within its walls. Anyone who wanted to leave the city to join the Romans was kept inside by the zealots; anyone sympathetic to the zealots had nowhere outside the walls to hide.

Vespasian was preparing to move his army from Cesarea to Jerusalem when word reached him of Nero's death (June 68) after a reign of thirteen years and eight days. Since it was possible his orders would be changed by the new emperor, Vespasian waited in Cesarea instead of continuing the war. Galba became emperor after Nero, reigning for only seven months and seven days before he was killed and replaced by Otho (January 15, 69). Affairs in Rome were so unstable during this period that the war against the Jews was temporarily turned into a holding action.

Simon

Simon the son of Giora, a young man born in Gerasa, had been driven out of the Acrabattene toparchy and joined the robbers at Masada before going off on his own and collecting a band of men in the mountains. They soon overran the villages in the mountains and many of the cities on the plain, growing from a collection of slaves and robbers into an army controlling a large area. Simon overran the Acrabattene toparchy as far as Great Idumea and built a wall around his base in the village of Nain. The caves in the Paran Valley were enlarged for use as a storage facility for his growing booty and a training site for his army. Simon made it no secret that he was preparing to assault the walls of Jerusalem.

To prevent him from growing any stronger, the zealots of Jerusalem attacked Simon and lost a great number of men before they were driven back into the city. Simon wasn't ready to tackle Jerusalem yet, so he turned his attention to Idumea and marched his army, now grown to 20,000, to its borders. The warlike Idumeans rapidly assembled an army of 25,000 and went to meet Simon. Although the battle lasted all day, there was no clear victory for either side, and both retired; soon Simon returned and pitched camp at Thecoe.

The Idumeans decided they needed a reliable estimate of Simon's strength before they met him in battle for the second time. Jacob, one of their commanders, volunteered for the mission with every intention of betraying the Idumeans, which he did as soon as he met Simon. He returned to his own army and gave them a false report indicating Simon was far stronger than he really was, then tried to convince the Idumeans it would be wiser to surrender the country than to oppose Simon. Once they were thoroughly frightened, Jacob sent for Simon, promising to disperse the Idumeans when he came. As Simon's army approached, Jacob and those with him fled, sending panic through the rest of the Idumean army and allowing Simon to march into Idumea without bloodshed.

Simon next took Hebron, an ancient city that had existed for 2,300 years — longer than the city of Memphis in Egypt. Hebron was said to be the home of Abram, the father of the Jews, after he had moved out of Mesopotamia. His family later moved from Hebron to Egypt, leaving behind fine marble monuments that still existed. Three-quarters of a mile outside of Hebron stood a large turpentine tree said to have been there since the creation of the world.

Simon laid waste to all Idumea to feed his forces, for besides his army, 40,000 others followed him, and he could not feed them all. Between his army's need for food and Simon's anger at Idumea, the country was nearly depopulated.

Simon's success worried the zealots so much that they laid a trap and captured his wife, bringing her back to Jerusalem, confident that Simon would lay down his arms to secure her safety. This only served to enrage Simon; he went to the wall of Jerusalem, encircled it, and vented his anger on anyone who ventured outside, armed or unarmed, torturing, killing, cutting the hands off a great many and sending them back into town to frighten the inhabitants. He told everyone he captured that he would take the city and kill everyone in it unless they returned his wife. The zealots released his wife.

As soon as Simon had his wife back, he returned to Idumea and brought its survivors back with him to Jerusalem, where he encircled the wall and resumed tormenting the city.

Now sedition and civil war broke out in Rome itself. Otho and Vitellius battled for the empire; after a reign of three months and two days, Otho killed himself, and Vitellius became emperor (April 69).

The Galileans

Within Jerusalem, the Galileans, whom John allowed to do whatever they wanted because of their loyalty to him, were running amuck. Their urge to plunder was insatiable; murder and rape were their common entertainments. They devoured their spoils and turned to feminine wantonness, decking their hair, dressing in women's clothing, painting their eyes. Not only did they look like women, they indulged in homosexuality and defiled the whole city, continuing to kill like men.

The Idumeans who still remained in the city rebelled against John, killing many of the zealots and driving the remainder into the royal palace where John lived and stored his booty. From there, the zealots were chased into the temple. The zealots who had been dispersed throughout the city joined the others in the temple and prepared to attack both the Idumeans and the citizens of the city.

The Idumeans and the citizens consulted with the high priests and decided to overthrow John by admitting Simon, who took the city peacefully in the third year of the war (April 69). Although John and the zealots were now trapped in the temple, they defended themselves from the top of the cloisters and battlements, holding their own and keeping Simon at bay.

Vespasian left Cesarea on June 5 to march against the cities of Judea that were not yet in Roman hands. He took the Gophnitick and Acrabattene toparchies and the cities of Bethel and Ephraim. Cerealis laid waste to Upper Idumea, took Caphethra and Capharabim, then captured Hebron. Now everything had been taken except the three fortifications being held by robbers: Herodium, Masada, and Macherus. Jerusalem was the only remaining rebel stronghold.

Vespasian Acclaimed Emperor

Returning to Cesarea, Vespasian heard that Vitellius had taken the office of emperor by force, which made him indignant and reluctant to continue the war against the Jews. Vespasian's commanders and soldiers met in several groups to discuss what was going on in Rome, then gathered together to proclaim him emperor of Rome and encourage him to save the government. Although Vespasian had been concerned for some time about the government, he preferred the safety of a private life to the dangers of holding office and refused to accept his troops' acclamation. At length, they convinced him they were serious, and Vespasian allowed himself to be acclaimed emperor by his troops in Judea (June 69).

Egypt

Knowing Egypt's wheat was vital to Rome's survival and that he needed to control that to depose Vitellius, Vespasian decided he had to take Alexandria. The two legions stationed there could then be joined to his army. Besides, if things went wrong during the struggle for power, Egypt would be an excellent defensive site for him.

On Egypt's west were the deserts of Libya. On the south, Syene divided Egypt from Ethiopia, and the impassable cataracts of the Nile were also to the south. On the east, the Red Sea extended to Coptus. The north was fortified by the land that reached to Syria and the portless Egyptian Sea.

Egypt's length between Pelusium and Syene was two hundred fifty miles; the sea passage between Plinthine and Pelusium was four hundred fifty miles. The Nile was navigable only as far as the city of Elephantine. The port of Alexandria was extremely difficult to enter from the sea, even during peacetime, its passage being narrow and full of submerged rocks. All in all, Egypt was an easily defended country.

Vespasian wrote to Tiberius Alexander, the governor of Egypt and Alexandria, telling him that his army supported his claim as emperor and asking for his support. Alexander readily agreed, as did the citizens of Alexandria, who all took an oath of loyalty to Vespasian. This gave Vespasian confidence in his claim, and he prepared to go to Rome. The news that Vespasian was emperor of the east spread rapidly, causing many cities to hold festivals and celebrations, and the legions in Mysia and Pannonia gladly took an oath to Vespasian.

Vespasian moved from Cesarea to Berytus, where he received many ambassadors from Syria and other provinces and met with Mucianus, the president of Syria, who gave him his support.

At this point, Vespasian remembered Josephus's prediction

that he would one day become emperor; he called together his advisers and set Josephus free of his bonds.

After appointing capable men to take office throughout the east, Vespasian went to Antioch to discuss where he should go next. He decided to send Mucianus to Italy while he went to Alexandria. Mucianus marched his army on foot through Cappadocia and Phrygia, since winter prevented a sea voyage.

In the meantime, Antonius Primus, the president of Mysia, sent a third of his legions to fight Vitellius. Vitellius sent out Cecinna, who had previously defeated Otho for the crown; he met Antonius near Cremona in Galatia, at the border of Italy. Cecinna saw that Antonius's troops were so well prepared and large in number that either fighting or retreating would be a mistake, so he decided to try and convince his army to desert to Antonius. At first they agreed, but later, after thinking over their decision, his men put him in bonds, to be returned to Vitellius as a traitor as soon as possible.

When Antonius Primus heard of this, he attacked immediately and drove Cecinna's army back toward Cremona, where he encircled them and took the city. Many foreign merchants and citizens died in Cremona, along with Cecinna's army of 30,200; Antonius lost only 4,500. Antonius freed Cecinna to carry the news of the victory to Vespasian, who received him with honor that covered the scandal of his treachery.

Vitellius's army met Primus's in three different engagements, losing over 50,000 men. Vitellius, drunk and full after a luxurious meal, wandered out of his palace, was drawn along and tormented by the Roman crowds, and finally beheaded on December 21, 69, after a reign of eight months and five days. The following day, Mucianus arrived in Rome with his army and ordered Antonius and his men to stop the indiscriminate killing that had been going on since their victory. He then produced Vespasian's son Domitian and recommended that the crowds let him hold the empire until his father could come and claim it.

Vespasian heard the good news in Alexandria and prepared to go to Rome, sending his son Titus to take Jerusalem and end the Jewish rebellion as soon as possible. Titus marched his army to Nicopolis, which was two and one-half miles from Alexandria, put them on boats, and sailed up the river along the Mendesian Nomus as far as the city of Thmuis. From there they marched through the cities of Tanis, Heracleopolis, Pelusium, Ostracine, Rhinocolura, Raphia, Gaza, Ascalon, Jamnia, and Joppa, to Cesarea.

FOURTEEN

Eleazar the son of Simon, who first separated the zealots from the people and led them into the temple and was jealous of John's growing power, revolted from him, taking with him Judas the son of Chelcias, Simon the son of Ezron, and Hezekiah the son of Chobar, all strong men who brought many followers with them. This group took possession of the court of the inner temple, making use of the consecrated food there and not venturing out very often because of their small number. The inner court was above the outer, which put John and his men at a disadvantage whenever they attacked Eleazar. Still, he continued his attacks, and Eleazar's men continued to sally forth against John until the whole temple was defiled by murders.

Now that the zealots were fighting among themselves, Simon the son of Gioras, who controlled all the upper city and most of the lower, decided to attack the temple, even though it was situated higher than his forces. This put John in the position of having to fight on two fronts at once. Simon's men he could repel with weapons thrown down by hand; to fight Eleazar, John had to use his many machines for throwing darts, javelins, and stones.

191

Although the zealots were impious men, they continued to permit priests and people into the temple to offer their sacrifices. But the darts John threw up against Eleazar fell with such force that they carried all the way to the altar, with the result that many priests and worshipers were killed and the bodies of foreigners lay mingled with those of the Jews, while blood lay in pools by the altar.

Anytime John was not under attack by Eleazar — which happened quite often because Eleazar's men were often drunk and tired — he sallied forth against Simon and the city. When John retreated, Simon attacked the city. In time, all the land around the temple became a wasteland and the city's stored wheat, which could have sustained it through a siege of many years, was all destroyed.

The innocent people of Jerusalem had no one to turn to and nowhere to flee, since the only thing all these factions agreed on was that no one was to be allowed out of the city. The people were unable to take care of their relatives, bury their dead, or mourn their city's destruction without fear.

Now John began cutting up the fine wood timbers Agrippa had stored in the temple in preparation for raising it another thirty feet. He made plans to use the wood for the building of towers that would reach above the inner temple's wall and allow him to fire down on Eleazar, but God prevented this by bringing the Romans against him before his towers could be built.

Titus's Army

Once he had assembled his forces, Titus began his march to Jerusalem, ordering others to meet him there. He had with him his father's three legions and Cestius's twelfth legion, which was anxious to avenge its former defeat at the hands of the Jews. The fifth legion was to come from Emmaus, the tenth from Jericho. Along with Titus marched the auxiliaries from the kings and a large force from Syria. Two thousand troops from Egypt replaced those who had been sent to Italy, while 3,000 men had been drawn from those guarding the Euphrates.

In addition, Tiberius Alexander joined Titus as a friend and adviser.

First in the line of march were the auxiliaries from the kings, followed by the road and camp builders. The commander's baggage was next with its guards, then Titus himself and his guards. After them came the pikemen and horsemen, followed by the machines of war, the tribunes and leaders of the cohorts, the flags and their trumpeters. The main body of the army followed, marching six deep in ranks, then their baggage and servants. Last were the mercenaries and the rear guard.

The army marched through Samaria to Gophna, where they stayed the night before marching on to the Valley of Thorns near the village of Gabaothsaul (the Hill of Saul), three and three-quarter miles from Jerusalem. There Titus selected 600 horsemen and went with them to scout the city and demand its surrender.

As long as Titus stayed on the road, no one appeared out of the city gates, but when he took his band of men off the road and down toward the tower of Psephinus, a crowd of Jews dashed out of the Women's Towers and came between Titus and his army. Trenches and gardens prevented him from going forward, so Titus turned his men and charged into the crowd, although he was not dressed in his armor. Two of his party were separated and killed, but the rest returned safely to camp.

As soon as the legion from Emmaus met the rest of the army, Titus moved his camp to Scopus, a plain on the northern quarter of the city less than a mile from the walls. Two legions camped there; the fifth legion camped about a half mile behind them. As these legions began to fortify their camps, the tenth legion arrived from Jericho and was ordered to build their camp on the Mount of Olives, a little less than a mile from the eastern side of Jerusalem. Between them and the city lay the deep Cedron Valley (Kidron Ravine).

The Jews Attack

The three factions within Jerusalem saw the Romans building three camps around their city and united for the sake of their common defense. Arming themselves, they attacked the tenth legion as it worked on its camp on the Mount of Olives. The legion had split into unarmed work parties and was caught by surprise; it was forced to run from the Jews storming out of the city.

Titus heard of the problem and immediately sent in troops to support the tenth legion. The Jews were driven down into the valley and back up the other side, where they continued the fight until noon, at which point Titus released the tenth legion to finish fortifying its camp while he and the other troops stayed to hold off the Jews.

Seeing the tenth legion climbing the Mount of Olives, the Jews decided they were retreating; new forces swarmed out of the city and through the Cedron Valley with such strength that no one could have stopped them. The Roman ranks with Titus scattered, leaving him and a small number of men alone. Titus flew into the Jewish forces around him. Meanwhile, the tenth legion on the mountain panicked, certain that the men with Titus would not have run if he hadn't, too. Eventually they saw Titus was still fighting, collected themselves, and went to his aid, driving the Jews back down the slope into the Cedron Valley. Now that the Romans again controlled their side of the valley, Titus sent the tenth legion back to finish their camp while he and the others protected them.

Passover

On April 14, 70, Eleazar opened the gates of the temple's inner court to admit everyone who wanted to celebrate the Passover. John took advantage of this opportunity to send in a large number of his men, most of whom were not purified and carried concealed weapons. Once in, they threw off their outer garments and revealed their armor and weapons, causing most of Eleazar's surprised men to flee to the temple's underground caverns. Many of the temple worshipers were trampled, beaten, and killed while John's forces seized the temple. Once he controlled the entire temple, John pardoned those of Eleazar's group who came out of the caverns, leaving only two factions fighting each other inside the city: Simon's and John's.

Titus Moves Camp

Titus decided to move his camps closer to the city's walls, assigning troops to keep the Jews inside Jerusalem while the rest of his men leveled the land in front of the city. They eliminated all the walls and hedges around the city's gardens, cut down fruit trees, filled up hollows and valleys, and tore down rocky cliffs until all the land between Scopus and Herod's monuments beside the Serpent's Pool was level and flat.

Now the Jews decided to try trickery on the Romans, sending some of their bravest men out from the Women's Towers as if they had been ejected from the city by those who wanted peace. Others on the walls threw stones down and called out to the Romans to come take the city, promising to open the gates for them.

Titus was reluctant to believe the men on the wall. Just the day before, he had had Josephus offer the city terms of peace without receiving an answer, so he ordered his soldiers to hold their ground. Some of them near the wall disobeyed and ran toward the gate. As soon as the Romans were between the two towers bordering the gate, the Jews ran out and encircled them, while those on the wall threw down stones and darts. Eventually the Romans repelled the Jews encircling them and ran off, while the Jews mocked them and beat on their shields in joy.

The returning soldiers were threatened by their commanders and Titus, who reminded them that the punishment for disobedience, whether it was successful or not, was death. The other legions crowding around begged Titus to be merciful in this case, which was already his inclination, since he thought it more fitting to punish individuals for disobedience, not whole groups. The men were let off with a stern warning.

The job of leveling the land in front of the wall had been completed in four days; Titus was anxious to move the army's baggage and those who followed the army into the safety of his camps as soon as possible. He set the strongest part of his forces in front of the northern and western parts of the wall, arraying them seven deep. Three ranks of footmen were placed ahead of these ranks, with three ranks of horsemen at the rear and seven ranks of archers in the middle. With these forces preventing the Jews from sallying out, Titus safely moved in his pack animals and the crowd following the army.

Titus and his legions set up their new camp a quarter of a mile from the tower of Psephinus, near the northwest corner of the wall. Another part of the army camped a quarter of a mile from the tower of Hippicus on the west of the city; the tenth legion remained on the Mount of Olives to the east.

The Walls of Jeusalem

Jerusalem was fortified with three walls, except in its impassable valleys, where there was only one wall. It was built on two hills with a valley between them. The hill containing the upper city was the higher of the two and was called the upper marketplace. The lower, crescent-shaped hill called Acra held the lower city. Next to Acra was a third hill, shorter than Acra and once separated from it by a broad valley. During the times of the Hasmoneans, this valley had been filled in, and the hill of Acra had been lowered so it would not be taller than the temple. Between the hills of the upper and lower cities, the Valley of the Cheese-mongers (Cheesesellers) ran as far south as the pool of Siloam. The outsides of these hills were impassable because of their deep valleys.

Of the three walls, the old one was hard to take because of the valleys and the hill rising above it, in addition to the fact that David, Solomon, and the kings after them built it very strongly. This wall began at the tower of Hippicus on the northwest side of the city and extended to Xistus, joined the council house, and ended at the temple's western cloister. Going the other way, it began at Hippicus, extended through Bethso to the gate of the Essens, went south to where it bent above Siloam, bent again toward the east at Solomon's pool, and reached as far as Ophlas, where it joined the eastern cloister of the temple.

The second wall began at the Gennath gate in the first wall and reached across the northern part of the city to the tower of Antonia.

The third wall began at Hippicus and ran north to the tower of Psephinus, turned east to the monuments of Helena, passed the sepulchral caverns of the kings, turned south at the Monument of the Fuller, and joined the old wall in the Cedron Valley. This wall, begun by Agrippa I, encompassed the newer parts of the city as it spread north of the temple and over a fourth hill, Bezetha. Bezetha lay near the tower of Antonia but was divided from it by a deep, man-made valley dug to protect the tower. Agrippa I had stopped building this wall just after its foundations were laid at the request of Claudius, but if it had been completed according to his plans, the city never could have been taken. The wall's stones were connected by stones 30 feet long and 15 feet wide. Since Agrippa's time, the Jews had built the wall to a height of 30 feet, then added 3-foot battlements and 4.5 foot turrets. The entire structure was 37.5 feet tall.

This wall's towers were 30 feet wide by 30 feet high, square and solid, with fine joints and stones as beautiful as those of the temple itself. Thirty feet up the towers were splendid rooms topped by upper rooms and cisterns collecting rainwater. The third wall had 90 of these towers, each 300 feet apart. The middle wall had 40 towers, and the old wall 60. The whole circumference of the city was a little over four miles.

The third wall's tower of Psephinus, where Titus pitched his camp, was 105 feet tall, its top providing views of Arabia at sunrise and the sea at sunset. Psephinus was built in the shape of an octagon. Nearby were the old wall's tower of Hippicus and two other towers, all three built by Herod the Great.

Hippicus, named for Herod's friend, was square. Its length and width were both 37.5 feet; Hippicus was 45 feet tall and solid. On top of the tower was a reservoir 30 feet deep. Over this sat a two-story house of 37.5 feet. Battlements of 3 feet and turrets of 4.5 feet topped the house, so the entire height of Hippicus was 120 feet.

The tower of Phasaelus, named for Herod's brother, was 60 feet wide by 60 feet deep by 60 feet tall. A 15-foot-tall cloister was built around the tower's top and covered by breastworks and bulwarks. A second tower, divided into many magnificent rooms, was built over the cloister, topped with battlements and turrets. Phasaelus's entire height was about 135 feet. Simon occupied this tower before the Roman siege.

The third tower was Mariamne. It was solid for 30 feet, 30 feet wide by 30 feet deep and 75 feet tall in total, with more luxurious apartments than those of the other two more strongly built towers.

Although these towers were tall, their sites made them seem even taller, as they were built on top of the old wall on a high hill. Each tower was made of perfectly joined white marble stones 30 feet long, 15 feet wide, and 7.5 feet deep.

Herod's Castle

Adjoining the towers of Hippicus, Phasaelus, and Mariamne was Herod's palace, entirely walled to the height of 45 feet and adorned with towers containing huge chambers, each capable of sleeping a hundred guests. These towers were built of a variety of rare stones, and the roofs were wonderful for the length of their beams and the splendor of their ornaments. The number of rooms in the castle was great, all filled with furniture and gold and silver vessels. In addition, the castle contained many porticoes, several groves of trees with long walks through them, deep canals, cisterns, and dovecotes. Just remembering this place is torment, for it was not destroyed by the Romans, but by the rebels at the beginning of the uprising. That fire began at the tower of Antonia, spread to the palace, and consumed the upper parts of the three towers.

The Temple

The temple was built on a strong hill that was enlarged as time went by but originally was protected only by the eastern wall and cloisters built by Solomon. Later, foundations were built up from the bottom of the hill on the other three sides and the upper and lower courts were walled. At its lowest, the wall reached up 450 feet from the valley; in other places, it was higher. The entire depth of the foundation was not visible once the valleys around the temple were filled to make them level with the city's streets.

Above the foundations were double cloisters with supporting pillars almost thirty-eight feet tall, each pillar made from a single stone of white marble. The roofs of the cloisters were of carved cedar; the outside was unadorned marble. The cloisters of the paved outer court were 45 feet wide and three-quarters of a mile in circumference, including the tower of Antonia.

When you went through these first cloisters into the second court of the temple, there was a 4.5-foot stone partition built all around, on top of which were equally spaced pillars declaring the law of purity, some in Greek and some in Latin, so no foreigner would go inside the sanctuary. The second court, or sanctuary, was fourteen steps above the first court, with its own wall. The buildings inside this square court rose 37.5 feet above the court. Beyond the 14 steps was a flat area of 15 feet leading to additional steps, each of 7.5 feet, which led to the gates. The north and south sides of the sanctuary each held four gates. The east side, which contained the women's court, had two gates. There were also women's gates on the north and south sides, through which there were passageways into the Court of Women, since they could not use the same gates as the men. The western part of this court had no gates at all. Between the gates, extending inward from the wall, was a single cloister.

Nine of the temple gates were covered on every side with gold and silver, as were their doorjambs and lintels, but one gate outside the inner court was made entirely of Corinthian brass and excelled the others. Each gate had two doors, each door 45 feet tall by 22.5 feet wide. Large rooms, built like towers, stood at the sides of each door and towered 60 feet high, supported by pillars 18 feet in circumference. All the gates were of equal size except for the Corinthian gate, which opened to the east. This was much larger, reaching up 75 feet with doors of 60 feet, and was adorned in a more costly manner than the other gates, with thicker plates of gold and silver.

The most sacred part of the temple, in the midst of the inner court, was reached by twelve steps. In front it was 150 feet high by 150 wide, though on its back it was 60 feet narrower. Its first gate was 105 feet high and 37.5 feet wide, with no doors because it represented heaven, which cannot be excluded from anywhere. Its front and walls were covered with gold; through it could be seen the outer part of the holy house, 135 feet tall, 75 feet long, and 30 feet wide. This gate also had golden vines above it, from which clusters of grapes as tall as a man hung down.

The inner part of the sanctuary appeared lower than the outer and had golden doors 82.5 feet tall by 24 feet wide. In front of these doors was a veil the same size, a Babylonian curtain embroidered with blue, flax, scarlet, and purple. The curtain's scarlet signified fire, flax the earth, blue the air, and purple the sea. The curtain also had embroidered on it all that was mystical in the heavens, except the twelve signs of the zodiac, which represented living creatures.

This part of the temple was 90 feet tall by 90 feet long by 30 feet wide. Its length was divided, and the first 60 feet contained three things famous among all men: the candlestick, the table of shrewbread, and the altar of incense. Seven lamps signifying the seven planets came out from the candlestick. The twelve loaves of shrewbread on the table signified the cycle of the zodiac and the year. The altar of incense, with its thirteen sweet-smelling spices, signified that God was the possessor of all things and all is to be dedicated to His use.

The most innermost part of the temple was 30 feet wide, separated from the outer part by a veil, and contained nothing at all. It was inaccessible and inviolable, and not to be seen by any: the Holy of Holies.

Around the sides of the lower part of the temple were many houses of three stories, with passages connecting them all. There were also entrances on each side into them from the gates of the temple. The whole temple height, including the 90 feet from the floor, amounted to 150 feet.

The outward face of the temple to the east was covered with gold plates that reflected brightly in the rising sun. From a distance, the temple looked like a snow-covered mountain. On its top, it had spikes with sharp points to prevent birds from landing on it and polluting it. Some of the temple's stones were 67.5 feet long, 7.5 feet high, and 9 feet wide.

Before this temple stood the altar, 22.5 feet high, 75 feet long, and 75 feet wide. It was built square, with corners like horns; the passage up to it was very steep. This altar was built without iron tools, and no iron was ever allowed to touch it. A partitioning wall made of fine stones stood 1.5 feet tall around the holy house and altar, to separate the people from the priests.

Anyone suffering from gonorrhea or leprosy was excluded from the city of Jerusalem. Women could not come to the temple during their periods and were never allowed beyond the women's court. Men or priests who were unpure were also excluded from the inner court.

All men from the priestly families who could not minister due to some defect of their bodies were allowed into the Court of the Priests, although they could not wear the sacred garments. Only the unblemished could approach the altar in fine linen. These men abstained from wine, to prevent themselves from accidentally transgressing the laws.

The High Priest

The high priest went up to the altar with the pure priests, not every day, but always during the Sabbath, new moons, and the festivals. When he officiated, he wore a pair of breeches reaching from beneath his genitals to his thighs; an inner garment of linen; a blue, seamless garment with a fringe reaching to his feet. Golden bells and pomegranates hung on his garment's fringe: the bells signified thunder, the pomegranates, lightning. The girdle that tied his garment to his breast was embroidered with five rows of various colors of gold, purple, and scarlet, also of fine linen and blue, as on the veil of the temple. The same type of embroidery was on his ephod, but the quantity of gold there was greater. Its shape was like that of a stomacher for the breast. Two golden buttons like small shields held the ephod to the garment. In these buttons were two very large sardonyxes carved with the names of the tribes. On the other part were hung twelve stones carved with the names of the tribes. These stones were a sardius, topaz, emerald, carbuncle, jasper, sapphire, agate, amethyst, ligure, onyx, beryl, and chrysolite.

A mitre of fine linen covered his head, tied by a blue ribbon encircled with another gold crown in which was engraved the sacred name of God. These vestments were worn only once a year, when the high priest went into the Holy of Holies; the rest of the year, his garments were simpler.

The Tower of Antonia

The tower of Antonia was located at the corner of the cloisters on the northern and western sides of the temple. It was built by Herod on a precipitous 75-foot rock. First the rock was covered with smooth stone. Next, a wall 4.5 feet high was built; within that wall, Antonia rose 60 feet high. The inside of the tower was like a palace, with rooms, courts, places for bathing, and broad spaces for camps. At each corner stood four additional towers, three of them 75 feet tall and the fourth, on the southeast corner, 105 feet tall. From the last tower, the whole temple could be seen.

On the corner where Antonia joined the temple cloisters, passageways, through which the Roman guards stationed in Antonia could pass to watch the temple, led to both cloisters.

FIFTEEN

The number of rebellious men in Jerusalem led by Simon and his fifty commanders was 10,000, not counting the Idumeans. Simon also controlled the 5,000 Idumeans with their eight leaders, among whom were Jacob the son of Sosas and Simon the son of Cathlas. John had 6,000 armed men under 20 commanders, plus Eleazar's 2,400 men. When Simon and John led their factions against each other, the city's citizens became their common prey.

Simon held the upper city and the great wall to the edge of the Cedron Valley, plus the old wall where it bent to the east from Siloam and went down to the palace of Monobazus. He also held the pool of Siloam and the lower city, plus all the city to the palace of Queen Helena.

John held the temple and the area around it, including Ophla and the Cedron Valley. Where their territories met, burned land served as their battlefields, for their warring did not end with the Roman encampment. The city never suffered any worse from the Romans than it suffered from John and Simon.

While the fighting continued inside Jerusalem, Titus took some horsemen to scout the walls and find a likely place to attack. He found no way accessible through the valleys and decided the best place would be at the monument to John the high priest, where the outer wall was at its lowest and not joined to the middle wall. This way also offered easy passage to the inner wall, through which he hoped to take the upper city and, through Antonia, the temple. As he was scouting the wall, Nicanor and Josephus attempted to talk to the defenders above them about terms of peace; Nicanor was wounded in the left shoulder by a dart. The Jews' refusal to listen to his ambassadors made Titus more determined to press on with his siege.

Titus gave his soldiers permission to burn the city's suburbs and ordered them to start collecting timber for raising banks against the wall. He divided his men into three parts to begin the banks, placing archers and those who shot darts nearby to protect the builders as they worked. In front of them he placed machines that threw javelins, darts, and stones, to prevent the Jews from sallying out or hindering the builders from the top of the wall.

Simon, who was near the site of the siege, set up the machines he had on the wall, although most of his men were unskilled in their use. They threw stones and arrows down on the Romans the best they could, while others sallied out by companies to fight. John stayed out of this action because of his fear of Simon, but he allowed his men to join in the attacks.

The Romans working on the banks covered themselves with panels for protection while their machines fought off the Jews. All the Roman machines were remarkable, but the ones of the tenth legion were extraordinary, capable of throwing darts and stones with such force that they could clear off the top of a city's walls. Seventy-five-pound stones could be thrown more than one-quarter of a mile by these machines.

At first the watchmen in the towers were able to see and hear the white stones as they approached and warned the people by yelling, "the son cometh," so they could move back and protect themselves. Soon the Romans began to blacken the stones so they could not be seen in advance and did great damage. Despite everything, the Jews continued to fight those raising the banks.

Upon finishing the works, the Romans measured the distance to the wall by throwing a lead and line and, finding the wall within range of their machines, brought them up to the bank and set them to work. The bombardment from three different Roman locations convinced those inside the wall to work together in defense of the city, so they laid aside their quarrels to throw torches and darts down on the machines and those manning them. The boldest of the defenders leaped out onto the panels over the machines, tearing them apart and attacking the soldiers that worked under them. Their boldness began to be too much for the Romans, so Titus sent in reinforcements and placed horsemen and archers around the machines to repel the Jews trying to burn them.

The wall held up under the bombardment. The fifteenth legion's battering ram moved the corner of one tower, but the wall near the tower was undamaged.

The Jews stopped their sallies beyond the wall for a while and the Romans, deciding the Jews were tired, resumed their work or returned to their camps. Suddenly, a large number of Jews came out of an obscure gate in the tower of Hippicus, carrying fire, and attacked the Roman fortifications. The fighting around the machines was so heavy it seemed the Jews would succeed in destroying the machines, until the soldiers from Alexandria and Titus himself joined the fight, driving the crowd back into the city.

After the battle, Titus had a captured Jew crucified in front of the wall to frighten the Jews, and John, the Idumeans' leader, was killed by a dart shot by an Arabian.

The Outer Wall Falls

Titus had ordered three towers built, each 75 feet tall, then placed on the banks for driving the defenders off the wall. About midnight of the next day, one of these towers collapsed with such noise that the Romans thought their camp was under attack and began to panic. Titus discovered the reason for the noise and calmed his men.

These towers caused the Jews a great deal of trouble, since

they were higher than the wall. The Romans could fire down on the Jews with the machines in the towers, but the Jews' darts couldn't reach the men in the towers. These towers were too heavy to be toppled, and their iron plating prevented the Jews from burning them. The Jews were forced away from the wall, which left the Romans free to use their battering rams, and the wall was breached by the ram the Jews had named Nico.

A great many of the defenders had grown tired and been given permission to sleep some distance from the wall. The Jews were not too concerned about the first wall, anyway, since there were still two more untouched walls defending the city. The Romans drove back the few defenders guarding the wall and entered through the hole on the fifteenth day of the siege, May 7, 70, demolishing a large part of the wall along with the northern parts of the city that Cestius had demolished earlier in the war.

Titus pitched camp within the city at the Camp of the Assyrians, having taken everything north of the city as far as the Cedron Valley. He then began his attack on the second wall. John and his men defended the wall from the tower of Antonia and the northern cloister of the temple, fighting the Romans before the monument of King Alexander. Simon's army defended the wall near John the high priest's monument and fortified it to the gate where water was brought into the tower of Hippicus.

The Jews made frequent sallies out to fight the Romans, but their lack of skill often resulted in their being beaten back to the wall. When they fought from the top of the wall, however, they were able to hold the Romans off. Neither side grew weary as the sallies and attacks on the wall continued day and night; the personal courage of both Simon and Titus encouraged their men to great heights of bravery. One of the Romans, Longinus, left his troop and threw himself into the midst of a large number of Jews fighting outside the wall, killing two of them before rejoining his own men.

Titus brought one of his machines to the middle tower of the north part of the wall, where a Jew named Castor lay in ambush with ten others. When the tower was shaken, he stood up, reached out his hand, and called for Titus to show him and his men mercy. Titus stopped the attack on the tower to allow Castor to speak; Castor pretended he wanted to surrender. This pleased Titus, who declared that he wished the rest of the city was as sensible as Castor. Now five of Castor's men began to declare they wouldn't surrender — in the meantime, Titus was delaying his attack. Castor sent word to Simon that he could hold off the Romans for some time this way while Simon decided what he wanted to do, and the eleven men continued to argue back and forth, some even pretending to kill themselves.

During this interval, someone shot a dart at Castor and wounded him in the nose. He promptly pulled out the dart, showed it to Titus, and complained of the attack. Titus reprimanded the dart thrower and told Josephus to go give his right hand to Castor as a pledge of his safety. Josephus refused, not convinced Castor was actually planning to surrender, but a deserter named Aeneas volunteered and approached Castor, who also claimed to have money with him that he wanted to surrender. As Aeneas approached, Castor threw a large stone at him; he missed Aeneas but hit another soldier. Titus realized he'd been taken in and put the battering ram back to work on the tower. As it began to give way, Castor and his men set fire to the tower and leaped through the flames into a hidden vault under the tower, leading the Romans to think they had bravely thrown themselves into the fire.

The Second Wall

Titus took the second wall five days after the first (May 12), entering where the wool merchants, the braziers, and the cloth merchants worked in narrow streets leading obliquely to the wall. If he had widened the breach in the wall and laid waste to the area, he might have taken the city without loss, but he refrained from damaging the city any more than was necessary to gain the goodwill of its people. His soldiers were not permitted to kill the city's residents or set fire to their houses, and Titus promised to give the people back all their possessions, hoping to preserve both the city and the temple.

The people of the city were happy to agree to Titus's proposals; the Jewish rebels took his humanity as a sign of weakness and threatened the people with death if they spoke of surrendering the city. The rebels attacked the Romans in the narrow streets and from the houses, some of them sallying out the upper gates against the Romans still outside the wall. As more and more Jews joined the battle, their knowledge of the narrow streets gave them a great advantage, helping them drive the soldiers out of the city. The retreating Romans were hindered in their escape by the narrowness of the breach in the wall; all of them inside the city might have been killed if Titus hadn't placed archers at the upper ends of the narrow lanes to give them some protection as they retreated.

This victory made the rebels inside believe the Romans would never venture inside the wall again and the city could be held as long as they stayed inside the wall. They could not see how strong the Romans really were or how close they themselves were to famine. They had been living off the misery of the city's citizens for so long that the people were beginning to die from starvation. This didn't seem to bother the rebels; it just meant more food would be available for them.

The Jews covered themselves with armor, made a wall of their own bodies against the breach in the wall, and held the Romans off for three days. But on the fourth day, they were forced to retreat, and Titus retook the wall, demolishing it totally and putting a garrison into the towers on the southern section of the city while he planned how to take the old wall.

The Famine Begins

Titus decided to relax the siege for a little while, in hopes the city would surrender as its supplies dwindled. It was time for his soldiers to be paid; he ordered the whole army drawn into battle array in sight of the city and had all the soldiers paid over a period of the next four days, while the city watched.

On the fifth day, he divided his legions and began to raise banks at the tower of Antonia and John's monument. He planned to take the upper city from the monument and the temple from Antonia, for if the temple were not taken, the city could not be held. Simon and the Idumeans attacked those building at John's monument; John's zealots fought at Antonia. The Jews occupied the high ground in this engagement and had learned how to use their machines — they had 340 stone-throwing machines in their possession — making the Romans' building difficult. As the work continued, Titus sent Josephus to speak to the defenders and encourage them to surrender, telling them their fight was doomed to failure by God. But they would not yield.

Although Simon and John cut the throats of anyone caught trying to leave the city, many still managed to escape and were then released by Titus. Those left behind were engaged in a constant search for food, as were the zealots, who searched the city's houses. Many of the people sold everything they had for one measure of wheat or barley, then locked themselves inside their houses to eat. The more powerful of the city still had more than enough food, but the weaker were dying daily. Children stole food from their fathers; mothers from their dying infants. The zealots used horrible tortures to force people to give up their hidden food, and those sneaking outside the walls at night to gather plants and herbs were met on their return by the zealots and their food confiscated.

The city's rich men were taken to the zealot leaders. Some were falsely accused of plotting or planning to desert; all were robbed. No other city ever suffered such miseries, nor did any age ever breed such a wicked generation. They confessed truthfully that they were slaves, scum, the spurious and abortive offspring of our nation, overthrowing the city themselves and forcing the Romans to gain a bad reputation by acting gloriously against them.

Now that the banks were nearly completed, Titus sent parties of horsemen to lay ambushes for those coming out of the city to gather food. Some of these people were fighting men, but most were poor people kept in Jerusalem by fear for their families. Forced to go out in search of food, they were in danger of being taken by the Romans. If they defended themselves against the Romans and fought them, it was too late to beg for mercy; they were whipped and tortured before they died, then crucified before the city's wall. Every day, at least 500 Jews were caught in this manner. Titus didn't feel he could let them go, but neither could he spare the men to guard them. In addition, he hoped the Jews would be frightened into surrendering by the sight of their dead, so the soldiers nailed one Jew after another to the crosses, until they ran out of crosses.

The rebels were not discouraged by the sight. Instead, they brought the relatives of those on the crosses to see their bodies, along with those who hoped to gain safety by surrendering to the Romans, and told them that was how the Romans treated anyone who surrendered. Still, many ran away, preferring death to starvation. Titus ordered the hands of many of those caught cut off, indicating they were not deserters, and sent them to John and Simon with a demand they save the city by surrendering.

The men replied that God would protect His temple and decide the outcome of the struggle Himself. They were not concerned with the city or the Romans' threats.

The Romans had begun raising their four great banks on May 12, finishing them with difficulty on May 29. One was raised by the fifth legion at the tower of Antonia, next to the middle of the pool called Struthius. The twelfth legion's bank stood about 30 feet from that of the fifth legion's. The tenth legion's was on the north quarter of the city at the pool of Amygdalon, while that of the fifteenth legion was 45 feet away at the high priest's monument.

Once the machines were in place on the banks, John undermined the bank by Antonia, then set fire to the mine's supports, collapsing the bank and rendering it useless to the Romans.

Two days later, Simon and his men boldly attacked the other banks, running out and setting the machines on fire. As the fire spread, the Romans came running from their camp to save the machines. They were beaten off and retreated toward their camp, which encouraged more and more Jews to join the battle, until they chased the Romans as far as their camp fortifications and engaged the camp's guards in battle.

Roman discipline was strict, especially for those assigned to protect the army's camps. Camp guards faced capital punishment if they deserted their posts for any reason, so the guards stood firm against the Jews, which encouraged the other soldiers to do the same. The camp's throwing machines were brought to its wall and used to prevent any more of the unarmored Jews from leaving the city and joining those attacking the camp, who were now engaging the soldiers in hand-to-hand fighting. The courage and boldness of the Jews drove the Roman defenders back farther and farther.

Titus returned to camp and reproached his men for allowing their own walls to be endangered by people suffering from a siege themselves; he took some troops and fell on the flank of the attacking crowd. The armies were now so intermingled and the dust and noise so great that no one could tell an enemy from a friend. After a fierce battle, the Jews retired to the city, leaving the Roman banks, built with great effort, demolished in the space of one hour.

The Roman Wall

Titus called his commanders together to decide what should be done next. Some advised that he storm the city wall with the whole army at once. So far, only parts of the army had attacked at various times. Others were for raising the banks again, while still others advised doing nothing and letting famine conquer the city for them.

Titus didn't think it fit to do nothing, yet saw it was wasteful to fight men who were already killing one another inside the walls. A lack of materials would make rebuilding the banks difficult, and it was almost impossible to prevent the Jews from sallying out of the gates. It would also be difficult to encircle the city with soldiers and prevent the Jews from smuggling in food to prolong the siege. Titus proposed building a Roman wall around the entire city to prevent the Jews from coming out. Once they were further weakened by famine, he would construct the banks against the wall.

Titus's wall began at his camp by the Camp of the Assyrians

211

and went down to the lower parts of Cenopolis, along the Cedron Valley to the Mount of Olives. It then bent southward to encompass the mountain as far as the rock of Peristereon and the hill next to it, to Siloam. Here it turned west and went down to the valley of the Fountain, after which it went up again at the monument of Ananus and encompassed the mountain where Pompey had once camped. Here it turned north to a village named "the House of the Erebinthi," encompassed Herod's monument, and joined Titus's camp on the east. The wall's total length was nearly five miles. Outside the wall, thirteen places were built for garrisons; the total circumference of these was one and one-quarter miles. This huge amount of space was walled in three days. Once the job was completed, Titus took the first watch of the night, Alexander the second, the commanders of the legions the third.

The Famine Intensifies

All hopes of escape were now denied the Jews. Famine began to destroy whole houses and families. Upper rooms filled with dying women and children, the city's lanes became choked with the bodies of the old, children and young men swelled with starvation and died in the marketplaces. The sick survivors were too weak to bury their dead. There was no lamentation or complaining in the city; starvation robbed everyone of emotion, leaving the city deathly quiet.

Even more terrible than the miseries of starvation were the acts of the robbers, who laughingly plundered the homes of the dead, defiled bodies with their weapons, and killed those who lay dying, while those who begged to be put out of their misery were left to suffer. Everyone who perished within the city died with his eyes fixed on the temple.

At first, the rebels ordered the dead buried out of the public treasury to keep down the stench. When that became impractical because of the large number of bodies, the dead were thrown into the valleys below the city. Titus, making his rounds of the valleys and seeing them filled with the dead, called God to witness that this was not of his doing.

212

The Roman soldiers had plenty of wheat and other food from Syria and the neighboring provinces and often stood near the city wall to flaunt their food in front of the starving. Still the city showed no signs of being ready to surrender, so Titus began raising his banks again, hoping to end the siege and save the innocent who still survived inside. Materials were hard to find, since all the trees nearby had been used for previous banks; soldiers brought in materials from as far as eleven miles away and raised four banks, much larger than the former ones, next to the tower of Antonia.

The Rebels

Inside the city, Simon condemned Matthias, the high priest who had convinced the people to open the gates to Simon, to death, along with three of his sons. Matthias begged to be killed first so he wouldn't see his sons die; Simon had him killed last and refused their bodies burial. The priest Ananias, the son of Masambulus; Aristeus, the scribe of the sanhedrim; and fifteen other notable men were also slain by Simon. Josephus's father was imprisoned, and everyone in the city was warned not to talk to him. Anyone who lamented the deaths of these men was immediately executed.

Judas the son of Judas, Simon's officer in charge of one of the city's towers, called together ten of his most faithful men and proposed they turn the tower over to the Romans before they were killed themselves. Judas called down to the Romans to offer them the tower; his offer was at first ignored. Just as Titus and his men approached, Simon took the tower and killed Judas and his men in Titus's sight. When he had mangled their dead bodies, he threw them off the wall.

As he was walking around the city one day, Josephus was hit in the head and rendered unconscious by a rock thrown from the wall. He would have been captured by the Jews who sallied out after him, if Titus hadn't sent troops to rescue him and take him back to the safety of the camp. Soon rumors spread throughout Jerusalem that he was dead. His imprisoned mother told her guards she had given up ever seeing her son alive after the siege of Jotapata; privately, she mourned his death. But Josephus soon recovered consciousness and re-appeared in front of the wall, calling out to those in the city to surrender, which encouraged the people but infuriated the rebels.

The Deserters

People still managed to desert the city whenever possible, either by throwing themselves off the wall or going out the gates as though they were attacking the Romans. Many of them, starved as they were, died from overeating as soon as they were taken by the Romans, not having the patience to slowly reaccustom their bodies to food. Others were killed by Arabians and Syrians looking for the gold that many deserters swallowed before leaving the city. In one night alone, 2,000 Jews were butchered for their gold.

When Titus heard of this, he gathered together all the commanders of the auxiliaries and of his own men (for some Romans were also guilty) and threatened to kill anyone caught butchering Jewish deserters for their gold. Still, the practice continued in secret. Once word reached Jerusalem, many people gave up their plans to desert.

Meanwhile, John was running out of people to plunder, so he took to sacrilege and melted down many of the temple's sacred utensils — caldrons, dishes, tables, vessels — many of them gifts from Roman emperors who respected the temple more than John, a Jew, did. John told his men it was proper to use divine things to fight a divine war; those protecting the temple were free to live off it. He emptied the vessels in the inner temple of their sacred wine and oil and distributed it to the crowds. If the Romans had delayed any longer in attacking these villains, the city would certainly have been swallowed up by the earth or flooded or destroyed by lightning, as Sodom was, for it had brought forth a generation more atheistic than those who had previously suffered such punishments from God.

At this time Manneus the son of Lazarus deserted to Titus and reported that he had counted 115,880 dead bodies being carried out of one gate between April 14 and July 1. Still more

214

had not been buried but lay in the city or had been thrown over the wall. Other Jews told Titus no less than 600,000 bodies had been tossed outside the gates and still more lay piled in heaps in the city's houses. Wheat was selling at an exhorbitant price in the city, and people were raking through dung piles for food.

The suffering of the city grew worse every day, until even the rebels began to suffer from the famine. The heaped-up bodies by the gates were such a horrible sight producing such a terrible smell that they hindered those sallying out against the Romans, although by now they were so used to death that they merely walked over the dead.

The Banks Rebuilt

Despite the difficulty they had in procuring materials, the Romans completed their new banks in twenty-one days. The Jews knew the city would be taken if they failed to burn the banks. At the same time, the Romans knew the scarcity of materials would make it impossible to rebuild the banks and take the city, if they were destroyed.

John and his men made plans for their own security in the event the wall was destroyed, then attempted to burn the banks before the battering rams could be brought up. But they didn't attack in great numbers and work together with their normal boldness and violence. Instead, they found the banks guarded all around by Romans willing to die to preserve them. The land in front of the banks was under heavy bombardment from the Roman machines. They retired without doing anything. This was on July 1.

The machines were brought up and set to work on Antonia, while the Jewish defenders threw darts and stones down from the tower. Although they were wounded by the stones, some of the Romans held their shields over their heads, undermined Antonia's foundation, and removed four of its stones. That night the wall was so shaken by the battering rams where John had previously undermined the Roman bank that the ground gave way and the wall suddenly fell.

Although they were dismayed by the fall of the wall, the Jews

215

were encouraged to see that the tower of Antonia still stood. The Romans soon discovered that John had built an unexpected new wall inside the one they had just breached. This new wall appeared to be fairly weak and was easy to climb onto over the ruins of the first wall, but the Romans were afraid to venture onto it. Titus encouraged his men, saying he realized those who climbed the wall first would be in great danger, but the wall in front of it was easy to climb and the new wall was weak. Those who died in the attempt would receive great rewards in heaven; those who climbed it and lived would be promoted.

Sabinus

Most of the Romans were still afraid of the danger involved. Sabinus, a Syrian by birth, who was known to be a brave man, was the first to rise up, although he hardly looked heroic. Sabinus was black, lean and thin, but his small body was far too thin to contain all the courage he possessed. He volunteered to be the first to die in climbing the wall. Holding his shield over his head with his left hand and drawing his sword with the right, he marched to the wall at noon, followed by only eleven others.

Those guarding the wall threw down darts and huge stones, but Sabinus never stopped until he reached the top of the wall and chased its defenders off. Just as he reached his goal, Sabinus tripped on a large stone and fell down with a good deal of noise. The Jews who turned back at the noise saw Sabinus was all alone on the wall and began throwing darts at him. He raised himself to one knee, covered himself with his shield, and wounded many of his attackers before he died. Three of his supporters were dashed to pieces by stones as they reached the top of the wall; the eight others were wounded but pulled off the wall by the Romans and taken back to camp. This happened on July 3.

The Capture of Antonia

Two days later, twelve Romans guarding the banks got together with the standard bearer of the fifth legion, one trumpeter, and two horsemen and quietly approached Antonia over the rubble during the night. After cutting the throats of the tower's first guards, they took possession of the wall and ordered the trumpeter to sound his trumpet. This chased off the remainder of the tower's guards before they even saw how few Romans there were.

Hearing the signal, Titus ordered his army readied and climbed the wall with his commanders. Some of the Jews fleeing toward the temple fell into the mine John had previously dug under the Roman banks. John's and Simon's armies fought together to keep the Romans out of the temple, knowing their cause would be lost if that were taken. Both sides fought at close quarters with their swords, hampered by the narrowness of the area from organizing into groups. The battle lasted from the night into the morning, the Jewish defenders becoming more numerous as time passed, while the Roman reinforcements failed to arrive. Eventually the Romans decided to be satisfied with occupying Antonia.

Julian

A centurion named Julian was standing by Titus at the tower of Antonia as the Romans began to give ground. He was from Bithynia, a man of great skill, strength, and courage, who enjoyed a good reputation within the army. By himself, he leaped out at the Jews and single-handedly made them retreat to the corner of the temple's inner court, killing everyone he could catch as they fled from him. Like every other Roman soldier, Julian wore shoes full of thick, sharp nails. As he ran on the smooth marble floor of the temple, he slipped and fell on his back in his armor, making a loud noise. The Jews gathered around him in crowds and struck at him, but the heavily armored Julian was not easy to kill.

Although Titus wanted to go to his aid, he was too far away. Those closer were too frightened by the crowd of Jews to attempt rescuing Julian. He struggled for a long time, wounding many who attempted to kill him, before his throat was finally cut. The Jews took up his body, put the Romans to flight, and locked them in the tower of Antonia. The bravest of the Jewish

217

soldiers in this battle were Alexas and Gyphtheus, from John's army; Malachias, Judas the son of Merto, and James the son of Sosas, from Simon's men; the two zealot brothers, Simon and Judas, the sons of Jairus.

SIXTEEN

On July 17, Titus ordered the soldiers with him inside Antonia to open the foundation wide enough so the army could enter the tower. Then he sent for Josephus, for he had heard that the daily sacrifice had not been offered at the temple because of a lack of men and that the people were upset by this failure. Josephus was instructed to tell John that if he wanted to fight, he would be allowed to bring his army out of the city and do battle without danger to the city or temple. He asked John not to offend God by defiling the temple and to allow the discontinued sacrifices to be made. Josephus delivered his message to John and all those close enough to hear him, with tears in his eyes and sobs of sadness for the city and her inhabitants.

Some people were still managing to escape the city and flee to the Romans. The high priests Joseph and Jesus escaped, as did three sons of Ishmael, four sons of Matthias, and the fourth son of the Matthias killed by Simon. Many of the nobility and priests also escaped. All were treated kindly by Titus and sent to live in the village of Gophna until the siege was over, at which time Titus promised he would return their possessions. These people happily moved to Gophna, but since they were not seen again in Jerusalem, the rebels told those inside the city they had all been killed by the Romans. This trick deterred many from deserting the city until Titus recalled the deserters from Gophna and had them show themselves to the people while urging them to surrender. Many more fled to the Romans.

Titus reproached John for defiling the temple and gave him one more chance to save it. "I do not force you to defile this your sanctuary; and if you will but change the place whereon you will fight, no Roman shall either come near your sanctuary, or offer any affront to it; nay, I will endeavor to preserve you your holy house, whether you will or not."

As Josephus translated for Titus, the rebels convinced themselves that Titus was speaking out of fear, not from goodwill, and they grew insolent.

Attack on the Temple

Titus could not bring his whole army against the temple at once, because space was so limited. He chose thirty out of every hundred soldiers, putting a thousand under each tribune with Cerealis as commander-in-chief and ordering them to attack the temple guards about the ninth hour of the night. He himself watched from the tower of Antonia, after his commanders dissuaded him from personally taking part in the battle.

The soldiers did not catch the temple guards asleep as they had hoped and were forced to fight them, thus bringing out the others within the temple. Darkness and confusion gave the Jewish defenders more difficulty than it gave the Romans, with the result that the Jews killed more of their own men than the Romans killed. Once it was light, both sides sorted themselves out and continued the battle in a more orderly fashion. Much of this battle was a stationary fight, where troops advanced a little, then moved back, since there was no room for flight or pursuit. The battle continued from the ninth hour of the night until past the fifth hour of the next day, with no clear winner.

Of Simon's men, Judas the son of Merto and Simon the son of Josias fought especially well. Of the Idumeans, James the son of Sosas and Simon the son of Cathlas were outstanding. John's leaders were Gyphtheus and Alexas, while Simon the son of Jairus was the most outstanding fighter of the zealots.

In the meantime, the rest of the Roman army had, over the last seven days, torn down some of Antonia's foundation and made a path into the temple. The legions approached the first court (the Court of the Gentiles) and began to raise their banks. The first bank was against the northwest corner of the Court of the Israelites. Another was at the northern edifice between the two gates. The third was raised at the western cloister of the Court of the Gentiles, the fourth against its northern cloister.

Two days after the Romans attacked the temple, many of the starving rebels got together to attack the Roman guards on the Mount of Olives at the eleventh hour of the day, hoping to catch them by surprise, but the Romans were warned and prevented them from getting over the wall between them. One of the Roman horsemen, Pedanius, a strong man in full armor, leaned down from his horse and caught one of the rebels by the ankle as he chased him down into the valley. Pedanius took the captured rebel to Titus, who complimented him on his strength and had the rebel killed.

The Cloisters

To hinder the Romans from coming into the temple from Antonia, the Jews now set fire to the northwest cloister where it joined the tower, then broke down about 30 feet of the cloister. Two days later, on July 24, the Romans set fire to the cloister again, burning nearly twenty-three more feet. The Jews then cut off the remaining roof, until the tower of Antonia was completely separated from the temple, making no attempt to stop the fire that was burning to their advantage.

There was at this time among the Jews a despicable common man with no character named Jonathan, who went out at the high priest John's monument and challenged the best of the Romans to single combat. No one saw fit to accept his challenge, so Jonathan called them all cowards and heckled them. A horseman named Pudens eventually ran out to meet Jonathan, and was on all accounts beating him until he fell down and Jonathan cut his throat. Jonathan then stood on

Pudens's body to exult over him and jest at the Romans; he was shot by a Roman dart and fell dead over Pudens's body.

The Jews in the temple continued to fight off the Romans on the banks. On July 27, they filled the roof of the western cloister of the Court of the Gentiles with dry materials, bitumen, and pitch, then retreated off the cloister as though they were tired. This encouraged many of the Romans to climb onto the cloister roof in pursuit, although most of the Romans held their places, not trusting this unusual Jewish retreat. The Jews then set fire to the roof.

One of the men trapped on the burning roof was named Longus, a man the Jews admired for his courage. They encouraged him to jump down into the temple, promising him safety if he did. But Longus's brother Cornelius persuaded him not to tarnish the glory of the Roman army or himself by saving himself in this manner. Lifting his sword in front of both armies, Longus killed himself.

Another soldier trapped on the roof, Artorius, called down to his tentmate Lucius, saying he would make him his heir if he would catch him as he jumped. Lucius was crushed into the pavement as Artorius jumped to safety on top of him.

This cloister was burned down as far as John's tower; the rest of it was cut off from the temple by the Jews after killing the Romans on top of it. The following day, the Romans burned down the entire northern cloister as far as the eastern cloister overlooking the Cedron Valley.

The Famine

The number perishing from famine continued to grow daily; war broke out over every piece of available food. The people's hunger was so great they were forced to chew anything they could find — belts, shoes, the leather from their shields, wisps of old hay.

A certain wealthy woman named Mary had fled to Jerusalem earlier during the war. Her father was Eleazar, from the village of Bethezub, which means "the house of hyssop." Everything she had brought with her from Perea had been stolen from her; now it was impossible for her to obtain even a scrap of food. In despair, Mary took up her infant son, who she felt had no future except that of a slave, and killed him. She then proceeded to roast him and eat half of his body, hiding away the rest. Smelling the meat cooking, some robbers came into her house to demand it from her. When she offered what was left to the robbers, they backed away in horror. She taunted them for being weaklings who couldn't bring themselves to do what a woman had done. Word of Mary's actions spread throughout Jerusalem, horrifying everyone in the city and making many wish they were already dead so they wouldn't know of these horrid deeds.

The Temple Gates

On August 8, two legions completed their banks, and the battering rams were set against the western side of the inner temple. For the past six days, the strongest of the Roman machines had bombarded the wall to no effect; now even the rams failed.

Other soldiers had undermined the foundation of the northern gate and removed the outer stones supporting it, but the inner stones continued to hold the weight of the gate. Giving up trying to dig or beat their way in, the Romans brought ladders and climbed to the top of the inner temple's cloisters, where the Jews met them in a fierce battle and forced them to retire after a great loss of life on both sides. Titus realized his attempts to spare the temple were costing him too many lives and ordered the gates set on fire.

The melting silver on the gates quickly carried the flames to the adjoining cloisters, which burned for the next two days while the Romans fired one section of cloister at a time. On the following day, Titus ordered the fires extinguished and a path cleared for the army while he met with his six principal commanders: Tiberius Alexander, the army's commander; Sextus Cerealis, commander of the fifth legion; Larcius Lepidus, commander of the tenth; Titus Frigius, commander of the fifteenth; Eternius, commander of the two Alexandrian legions; Marcus Antonius Julianus, procurator of Judea. Some of

223

these men believed the temple should be destroyed no matter what happened; others said it should be destroyed only if it were used as a citadel. Titus decided to try to save it, if at all possible.

The next day, a great number of Jews made a sudden sally out of the eastern gate and attacked the Romans guarding the Court of the Gentiles. Titus sent horsemen in to help the guards, who were being overwhelmed by the fury of the Jewish attack; eventually, the Jews had to retreat and lock themselves into the inner court of the temple.

The Temple Burns

Titus retired to the tower of Antonia on August 10 and resolved to storm the temple early the following morning with his whole army. But once he was gone from the temple, the Jews attacked the Romans attempting to put out the fires. As the Jews were being forced back inside the temple, a Roman soldier picked up some burning material and, lifted up by a second soldier, set fire to a gold window that led to a passageway on the north side of the holy house. The Jews set up a loud clamor and ran to defend the temple.

When Titus heard of the fire, he ran to the temple with his commanders and several legions of troops and tried to order the fire extinguished. The Roman troops either could not hear his command or chose to ignore it in the heat of the battle. The Jews were losing on all sides, while many innocent people in the temple had their throats cut. Dead bodies lay heaped about the altar, and the pathway to it ran with blood.

Unable to control his troops, Titus entered the burning temple and found the inner rooms still intact. Liberalius was ordered to restrain the soldiers and have the fires put out before they spread to the inner rooms, but nothing could stop the soldiers now. Titus and his commanders retired when the inner rooms caught fire.

The temple was burned on August 10, exactly the same day it was burned by the Babylonians. Between the laying of the first foundation by Solomon and this destruction during the second year of Vespasian's reign was 1,130 years, 7 months, and 15 days. From its second building by Haggai in the second year of Cyrus the king until its destruction by the Romans were 639 years and 45 days.

The holy house was plundered as it burned, and 10,000 people were slain, regardless of age or condition. The noise arising from the city was immense, the cries of the Roman legions and Jews surrounded by the fires, the mourning of the people, and the roar of the fire all combined in one loud lamentation that reverberated off the mountains around the city. The area around the temple became covered with so many bodies that it was impossible to see the ground itself. Those rebellious Jews still alive fought their way out of the temple and down into the city itself, while the people who had gathered in the temple fled to the cloisters of the outer court.

At first, the priests took up the spikes that fell from the top of the temple and used them as darts against the Romans, but they were eventually forced back to hiding places on the twelve-foot-wide wall by the fire. Two of them — Meirus the son of Belgas and Joseph the son of Daleus — threw themselves down into the fire.

The Romans decided it was useless to try to save the many buildings outside the temple and burned everything, including the temple treasury containing the entire wealth of the Jewish nation. The soldiers then went to the remaining cloisters of the outer temple, where about 6,000 people had fled, and set the cloisters on fire, killing all 6,000.

Signs and Portents

The people had gone to the temple that day at the urging of a false prophet controlled by the rebels who had promised them signs of their deliverance. But they had ignored the signs they had already been given of the coming destruction. A star resembling a sword and a comet had stood over the city for a whole year.

Even before the rebellion began, there had been warning signs. Once when great crowds filled the temple for the April 8 celebration of Passover, a great light shone around the altar and holy house for half an hour during the night. Although some took this as a good sign, the sacred scribes read it as a bad one. At the same festival, a heifer being led to sacrifice by the high priest gave birth to a lamb in the midst of the temple. And the eastern gate of the temple, which was so large it took twenty men to close it and bolt it shut, opened by itself about the sixth hour of the night. The men of learning believed this meant the security of the holy house had been given up by the temple itself, and the gate had opened to receive the enemies of the Jews.

A few days after, on May 21, just before sunset, chariots and soldiers in armor were seen running among the clouds and surrounding cities. And during the feast of Pentecost, priests going into the inner court at night felt the earth tremble, heard a great noise, then heard a multitude of people crying, "Let us remove hence."

Four years before the war began, when the city was enjoying peace and prosperity, Jesus the son of Ananus, a plebian farmer, came to the feast where everyone made tabernacles to God in the temple. He suddenly began to cry out, day and night throughout the city, "A voice from the east, a voice from the west, a voice from the four winds, a voice against Jerusalem and the holy house, a voice against the bridegrooms and the brides, and a voice against this whole people!" Even though he was beaten, he continued his mournful warning. He was brought before Albinus, the Roman procurator, and whipped until his bones were laid bare, but his only words were, "Woe, woe, to Jerusalem!" Albinus dismissed him as a madman, but he continued his mourning, speaking nothing but this lament for seven years and five months, until the seige. During the seige, as he was going around on the wall, he cried out, "Woe, woe, to the city again, and to the people, and to the holy house!" Just as he added, "Woe, woe, to myself also!" he was killed by a stone from a Roman machine.

If anyone thinks about these things, he will find that God takes care of us and shows us how to preserve ourselves, but we perish by the miseries we bring on ourselves.

226

When the Jews demolished the tower of Antonia, they made the temple square, fulfilling the prophecy that the city and temple would fall once the temple was square. What most helped the people understand this war now was an ambiguous oracle found in the sacred writings who said, "about that time, one from their country should become governor of the habitable earth." This oracle certainly meant Vespasian, who was appointed emperor while in Judea. However, no one can escape his fate, even if he sees it beforehand.

Titus Meets With the Jews

Now that the rebels had fled into the city and the holy house had burned, the Romans brought their flags to the temple and set them up on the eastern gate, offering sacrifices to them and declaring Titus victorious with exclamations of joy. Those soldiers had collected so many spoils from their plundering that a pound of gold now sold for half its former price throughout Syria.

The Jewish rebels left in the city sent word that they would like to talk with Titus. Titus and his men stood on the western side of the temple's outer court, on one side of a bridge connecting the upper city to the temple. Simon and John stood on the other side of the bridge with their men about them. As the victor, Titus appointed the interpreter and spoke first. He reminded the Jews that they had chosen to rebel after being fairly treated by the Roman government and by himself. He had tried on many occasions to save the city and the temple, and he treated those who left the city humanely. And now they came to him in their armor to talk of forgiveness? Still, if they would throw down their arms and surrender, he would be mild, only punishing the guilty and saving the rest for his own use.

The Jews replied that they could not surrender because they had taken an oath not to, but if he would allow it, they would take their families and go into the desert, leaving the city to him.

It made Titus furious to have defeated men proposing terms to him as if they were victors. He warned them he would accept no more deserters from their ranks. From then on, they would all be treated according to the rules of war, and no one would be spared.

Titus gave his troops permission to plunder and burn the city. The following day, they set fire to the city archives, Acra, the council house, and Ophlas. The fires spread as far as Queen Helena's palace in the middle of Acra.

The same day, the sons and brothers of Izaates the king, together with many others from the city's nobility, asked permission to surrender. Although he was angry with everyone in the city, Titus let them live as captives, intending to take Izaates's sons and relatives back to Rome as hostages.

The rebels took the royal palace back from the Romans, killing and plundering the 8,400 people who had gone there with their possessions in search of refuge.

The following day, the Romans drove the robbers out of the lower city and set everything as far as Siloam on fire, but they found no plunder there, because the robbers had already taken everything to the upper city. Josephus continued to encourage the remaining rebels to surrender, but they dispersed themselves throughout the city's ruins and continued to kill anyone they caught trying to escape to the Romans. The only remaining stronghold for the Jewish rebels was the city's underground caverns, where they hoped they could hide until the Romans left.

The Upper City

On August 20, Titus decided the well-fortified and steep upper city could not be taken unless he raised banks against it. The four legions began building against Herod's palace, while the auxiliary troops built at Xystus as far as the bridge and the tower Simon had built against John.

The commanders of the Idumeans now sent ambassadors to Titus, asking him to let them surrender and live. Since much of the Jews' fighting depended on the Idumeans, Titus agreed to receive them, but Simon heard of their plan, killed the ambassadors to Titus, imprisoned the Idumean leaders, and had the troops watched. Many of them still managed to escape and surrender, although many were killed in the attempt. The Romans accepted those who surrendered, hoping to receive a good price for the Idumeans when they sold them as slaves, since they now had so many people to sell that the price they received had dropped drastically.

On September 7, the banks around the upper city were finished and the machines brought against the wall. As soon as the wall was first breached, the Jewish rebels fled the upper city, abandoning to the Romans what they might never had been able to take because of the strength of the upper city's towers.

The rebels fled to the valley below Siloam, throwing themselves against the wall the Romans had built, hoping to escape the city. Not able to prevail against the Romans at the wall, they broke up and hid in the underground caves.

Meanwhile, the Romans reached the top of the upper city's wall without bloodshed, only to find no one waiting to oppose them on the other side. They began killing those left behind, looting, and burning, although when they came to houses filled with the dead, they left them alone. Although they had respect for the dead, they had no mercy on the living. Blood ran down the narrow lanes in such quantity that it put out fires consuming many houses. By September 8, the whole upper city was in flames.

When Titus went into the upper city and saw the strength of the three towers (Hippicus, Phasaelus, and Mariamne), he thanked God that he hadn't been forced to try to take them, for he knew he couldn't have done it. Everyone imprisoned by the rebels in the upper city was freed, and the three towers were left standing as a monument to Titus's good fortune.

The People of Jerusalem

Titus now ordered that the people of the city be spared; his soldiers should kill only those fighting them with arms and should take the rest captive. The aged and the infirm were still killed, but anyone who seemed useful was locked within the walls of the Court of Women and his fate decided by Fronto, one of Titus's freedmen. Fronto killed all who were identified as rebellious or robbers. The tallest and most beautiful of the young men were saved for the triumphal procession; everyone else over the age of seventeen was sent in bonds to work the Egyptian mines. A great number were also sent into the provinces to provide amusement in the theaters. Those under seventeen were sold as slaves. In the days it took Fronto to make these decisions, 11,000 of the Jews died from starvation.

The number taken captive during the whole war (seven years) was 97,000. The number perishing during the siege was 1.1 million, most of them Jewish, but not from Jerusalem. Most of the victims had come to Jerusalem for Passover, been trapped there, and died from plague and famine.

Before the war, Cestius had asked the high priests to count the number celebrating the Passover feast. They counted 256,500 sacrifices, which amounted to 2,700,200 purified worshipers. Also in the city at that time would have been many who were impure, women, and foreigners who could not partake of the feast. This vast multitude coming from remote places was encompassed by the Romans and imprisoned within the city. The number of deaths exceeded all previous destructions by God or man.

As John and his men began to starve in the caverns, John begged Titus for permission to surrender; he was allowed to live as a perpetual prisoner. Simon struggled hard but eventually surrendered. He was saved for the triumphal procession in Rome and then killed. The Romans burned down the outskirts of the city and entirely demolished its walls.

Jerusalem was taken on September 8, 70. It had been taken five times before (six, counting Ptolemy); this was its second destruction. Those who took the city before but preserved it were: Shishak, the king of Egypt; Antiochus; Pompey; Sosius, and Herod. Before all these, the king of Babylon captured and destroyed it 1,468 years and six months after it was built. He who first built it was a powerful Canaanite named Melchisedek, called the Righteous King, which he truly was. He was the first priest of God and the first to build a temple there, changing the city's name from Salem to Jerusalem.

David, the king of the Jews, took the city from the Canaanites and settled his own people there until the city was demolished by the Babylonians 477 years and 6 months after David. Between David and the destruction of the city by Titus were 1,179 years. Between its first building and its final destruction were 2,177 years.

Neither its great antiquity, its vast riches, the spread of its people over all of the earth, nor the veneration paid to it could preserve Jerusalem from destruction. And thus ended the siege of Jerusalem.

INSPIRATIONAL LIBRARY

Beautiful purse/pocket size editions of Christian classics bound in flexible leatherette or genuine bonded leather. The bonded leather editions have gold edges and make beautiful gifts.

THE BIBLE PROMISE BOOK   Over 1000 promises from God's Word arranged by topic. What does the Bible promise about matters like Anger, Illness, Jealousy, Sex, Money, Old Age, et cetera, et cetera.

Flexible Leatherette . . . .$ 3.95
Genuine Bonded Leather $10.95

DAILY LIGHT   One of the most popular daily devotionals with readings for both morning and evening. One page for each day of the year.

Flexible Leatherette . . . .$ 4.95
Genuine Bonded Leather $10.95

WISDOM FROM THE BIBLE   Daily thoughts from the Proverbs which communicate truth about ourselves and the world around us. One page for each day of the year.

Flexible Leatherette . . . .$ 4.95
Genuine Bonded Leather $10.95

MY DAILY PRAYER JOURNAL   Each page is dated and has a Scripture verse and ample room for you to record your thoughts, prayers and praises. One page for each day of the year.

Flexible Leatherette . . . .$ 4.95
Genuine Bonded Leather $10.95

Available at your friendly Christian bookstore,
a wonderful place to visit!
or order from:
Barbour and Company, Inc.
P.O. Box 719
Uhrichsville, OH 44683

If you order by mail add $1.00 to your order for shipping.
Prices subject to change without notice.

IL